MARVEL AGE OF COMICS

WOLVERINE: WEAPON X

AN EXPLORATION BY

JIM RUGG

BLOOMSBURY ACADEMIC
NEW YORK • LONDON • OXFORD • NEW DELHI • SYDNEY

BLOOMSBURY ACADEMIC
Bloomsbury Publishing Inc, 1359 Broadway, New York, NY 10018, USA
Bloomsbury Publishing Plc, 50 Bedford Square, London, WC1B 3DP, UK
Bloomsbury Publishing Ireland, 29 Earlsfort Terrace, Dublin 2, D02 AY28, Ireland

BLOOMSBURY, BLOOMSBURY ACADEMIC and the Diana logo are trademarks of Bloomsbury Publishing Plc

MARVEL PUBLISHING
Jeff Youngquist, VP, Production and Special Projects
Brian Overton, Manager, Special Projects
Sarah Singer, Editor, Special Projects
Jeremy West, Manager, Licensed Publishing
Sven Larsen, VP, Business Development and Licensed Publishing
David Gabriel, VP, Comic Sales and Content Planning
C.B. Cebulski, Editor in Chief

BLOOMSBURY ACADEMIC
Haaris Naqvi, Global Editorial Director
Leah Babb-Rosenfeld, Editorial Director
Hali Han, Assistant Editor
Ian Buck, Deputy Head of Production
Zeba Talkhani, Senior Production Editor
Ben Anslow, Senior Designer

First published in the United States of America 2026

Cover Art by: Barry Windsor-Smith
Cover design: Ben Anslow

A catalog record for this book is available from the Library of Congress.

ISBN: PB: 979-8-7651-3876-2
ePDF: 979-8-7651-3879-3
eBook: 979-8-7651-3878-6

Series: Marvel Age of Comics

Typeset by RefineCatch Limited, www.refinecatch.com
Printed and bound in the United States of America

For product safety related questions contact productsafety@bloomsbury.com.

To find out more visit www.bloomsbury.com/marvel-books

CONTENTS

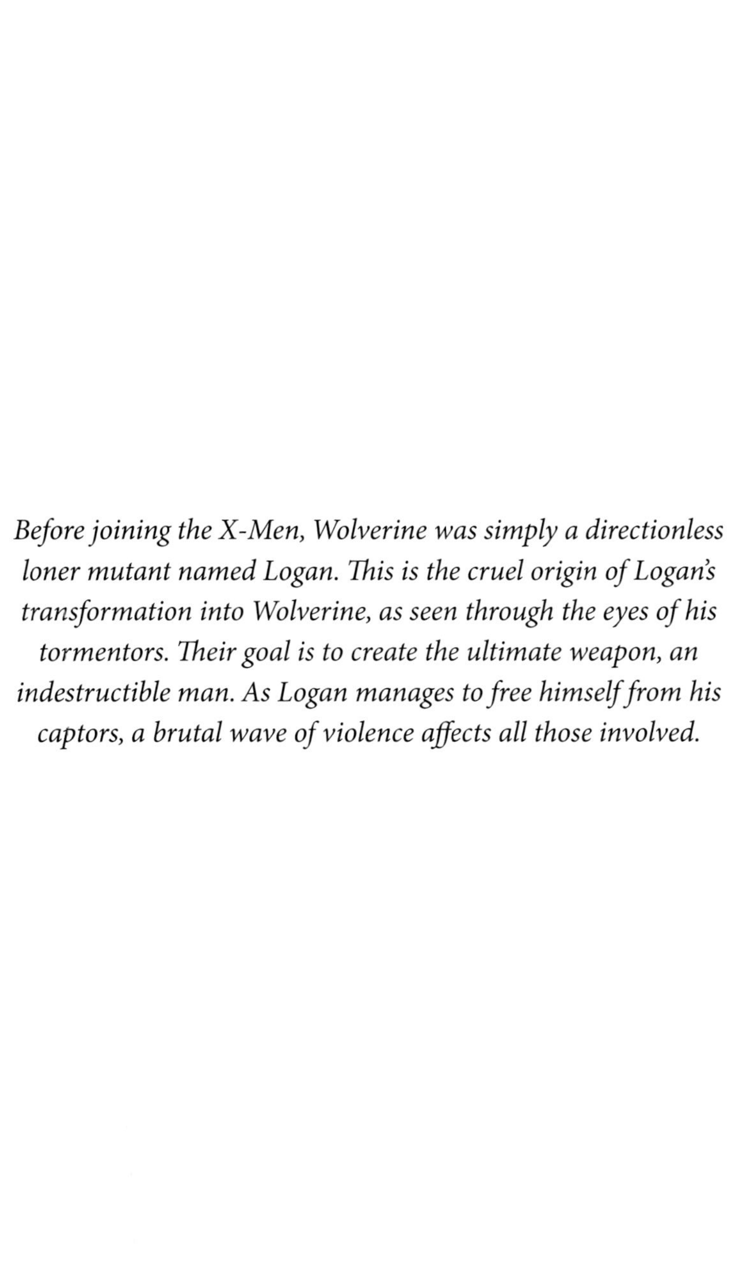

Before joining the X-Men, Wolverine was simply a directionless loner mutant named Logan. This is the cruel origin of Logan's transformation into Wolverine, as seen through the eyes of his tormentors. Their goal is to create the ultimate weapon, an indestructible man. As Logan manages to free himself from his captors, a brutal wave of violence affects all those involved.

PROLOGUE

I'll never forget the first time I saw *Weapon X*. It was early 1991. *Comics Scene* magazine, number 18, featured a preview article about it.

To understand the impact of Barry Windsor-Smith's *Weapon X*, I must start in the fall 1989. That's when I started reading comic books and declared that I wanted to be a comic book artist. After wondering why the Hulk was gray, curiosity got the best of me and I finally bought my first comic book—*Marvel Comics Presents* 26 from the local drug store. It looked like the characters I was drawing in my notebooks. I studied that book closely and saw credits for artists. By the time I got home, I knew what I wanted to do for the rest of my life—draw comic books.

I'm not sure what I bought next. It was either *Wolverine* 10 from a gas station at the bottom of the mountain where I lived. Or it was *How to Draw Comics the Marvel Way* by Stan Lee and John Buscema. I may have bought them on the same day. I remember *Wolverine* 10 felt a million times better than *Marvel Comics Presents* 26. I looked at the credits. John Buscema, penciller and Bill Sienkiewicz, inker! The same guy who drew *How to Draw Comics the Marvel Way*!?! Also, the back cover by Kent Williams—WOW!

For the next several years I continued to buy *Wolverine* comics (as well as any others I could afford and find). For the rest of my life, I always checked who the artist was and if I liked the art enough, I followed the artist.

Marc Silvestri was drawing Wolverine in *X-Me*n with gorgeous inks by Dan Green. Jim Lee drew an excellent Wolverine guest-star in *Punisher War Journal* and soon took over *X-Men*. John Byrne drew a story arc of *Wolverine* and made him so hairy it was kind of disgusting but also badass. Mike Mignola drew Wolverine in his iconic style in *Jungle Adventure*, while Rob Liefeld's Wolverine fought with Cable in *New Mutants*! Frank Miller drew the *Wolverine* mini-series. Fortunately, I found an affordable trade paperback of that one. Todd McFarlane drew Wolverine in *Hulk* and *Spider-Man* and Art Adams drew him in *Fantastic Four*.

I studied every Wolverine artist that I could find and their different art styles. Whether they made him look short enough. How they drew his claws or body hair or weird haircut. I would copy them in my sketchbooks and soon I drew him without copying by incorporating all of my favorite artist's ticks and techniques.

It was under these conditions that I came across a copy of

Comics Scene magazine in early 1991. "WOLVERINE: When he was wild!" in bold, bright yellow letters on a red background topped the magazine. That was enough for me. I turned to page 22 and my young comic brain expanded!

> Secrets of Weapon X
> Brushing continuity aside, Barry Windsor-Smith reveals the naked truth about Wolverine.

Like many comic book fans, Wolverine was my favorite character at the time. And one of the most unique elements of Wolverine's character was that his past was completely unknown! No one knew how he got those claws, how old he was, or whether Logan was his first or last name. He was a mystery. According to *Comics Scene* magazine—that was about to change! *Weapon X* would reveal Wolverine's secret origin!

The article was the first time that I had heard of Barry Windsor-Smith and I fell in love with his artwork at first sight! I was 13 years old. I wanted to be a comic book artist. Comic books were my obsession. I studied the article and read and reread it. The artwork that *Comics Scene* included in the article looked like nothing I had ever seen before! Pure excitement. Intricate, stylized anatomy. I quickly tried to copy the images in my sketchbook. Windsor-Smith's anatomy twisted Wolverine in ways I thought were impossible. His breathtaking line work was full of cross-hatched detail. I bought *Marvel Comics Presents* 72 the day it was released.

Since then, I have become a comic book artist, and writer, letterer, colorist, publisher, designer, teacher, YouTuber, collector, and critic…I've won an Eisner, an Ignatz, and an AIGA 50/50 medal. But I never forgot Barry Windsor-Smith's *Weapon X*. Thirty-five years after its first publication, it remains one of my favorite comics experiences and continues to inspire me.

1

Naked + Deadly

A naked, hairy man screams and howls as he kills a hallway full of guards. Long, bloody claws extend from his hands. Blood splatters the walls and the killer.

This is not an R-rated slasher movie filled with gratuitous violence, it is a Marvel super hero comic book from 1991 called *Weapon X* and the naked, blood-drenched killer is Wolverine, one of Marvel's most popular characters. *Weapon X* is Wolverine's origin story. And what an origin story it is—completely unlike any other Marvel comic book before or since.

By the late 1980s and early 1990s, comic books and comic book readers were changing. The average age of readers was going up and comic book storytelling was evolving to meet the demands of this expanding demographic. Changes can be seen in both writing and artwork including better characterization, more complicated plots, and improved production quality and artistic detail. Many "mature" comic books, especially those in the super hero genre, responded to this new direction with increasing levels of violence.

Even by the new standards of mature comics, Barry Windsor-Smith's *Weapon X* was extreme. Imagine trying to convince an editor, whose primary job is caretaking licensed children's characters, that the new Wolverine costume is his birthday suit with some decorative blood splatter.

Weapon X was serialized in 13 chapters in *Marvel Comics Presents* 72–84 published from March 15, 1991 to September 5, 1991.

An important element of the super hero genre is costuming. In *Weapon X*, Wolverine's costume is no clothes. You know what is more terrifying than a killer with giant claws? A NAKED killer with giant claws! The boldness and impact of this choice cannot be overstated. In many ways, *Weapon X* is the opposite of a super hero comic. It is a punk rock manifesto against the super hero genre! And not a subtle one, as Weapon X's costume attests.

In the 1980s, the super hero genre experienced a revisionist movement. Comics like *Watchmen*, *Elektra: Assassin*, *Miracleman*, *Marshal Law*, and *Bratpack* began to explore the social and psychological effects of super heroes through a more adult and, some might say, cynical lens. Creators deconstructed the super hero genre in order to mine new ideas, themes, and stories for an aging, maturing audience. Whether these comics specifically influenced Windsor-Smith is unclear but the concept of the super hero and the genre evolved through these works and *Weapon X* displays a similar approach with its experimental, challenging storytelling and complex, graphic presentation. Today comic books, graphic novels, and manga exist for every age group and subject imaginable. They can be found in bookstores, libraries, schools, and screens. Marvel Comics characters populate toy stores, movie screens, video games, TV, T-shirts, and more. Despite the mainstreaming of super heroes and the myriad interpretations that have spawned as a result, *Weapon X* still feels shocking, cutting-edge (no pun intended), and different than anything else that Marvel Comics has done! Decades after its initial publication, its impact remains potent.

Like film, painting, or photography, comics are an art form. In *Understanding Comics*, Scott McCloud describes the art form like a language. Within the art form of comics, several genres have emerged—memoirs, non-fiction, romance, crime, horror, and super hero. The super hero genre dominated the American comics market from the mid-1960s–2000s. In the 1950s, comic books were accused of contributing to the rise of juvenile delinquency. There were Senate subcommittee hearings on whether comic books were a threat to America's youth. After these hearings, the industry began regulating itself through an organization known as the Comics Code Authority. The Comics Code Authority was a review board. They created a code of decency and reviewed comic books. If the comic book passed the Code's approval, a Comics Code Approval seal was printed on the cover. This seal was intended to show parents which comics books were suitable for children. As a result, news-stand sellers refused to stock comic books that did not bear the Code's stamp of approval. The one exception was Dell, who licensed Disney characters for comic book publication and prided themselves on their own high-quality, morally upright standards. Between the negative press of the congressional hearings and the adoption of the Comics Code, the art form of comics was relegated to trash culture status suitable only for barely literate children. However, the art form continued and the super hero genre came to dominate it with their cast of do-gooders and Comics-Code-Authority-approved values. Characters like Spider-Man, the Hulk, Batman, and Wonder

Woman proliferated as comic books were deemed a children's medium, at least in America. The comics scene was quite different in Europe and Japan, but there were very few imports and translations from these places prior to the 1980s.

Meanwhile, in the 1960s and 1970s, American underground cartoonists like Robert Crumb and Trina Robbins created comix that used the art form to explore more mature, adult ideas. These underground artists proved that comics were a vital art form capable of handling any subject matter and expressing an infinite emotional range. This led to groundbreaking works in the 1980s such as Art Spiegelman's Pulitzer Prize-winning graphic novel *Maus*, the Hernandez' Brothers' *Love and Rockets*, and even dense, complex super hero epics like Frank Miller's *Dark Knight Returns*.

With *Weapon X*, comic book writer/artist Barry Windsor-Smith approached Wolverine not as a children's super hero book but rather as an opportunity to tell a story about horror, violence, and trauma. Wolverine is a killer with a mutant healing factor. That means his origin must contain trauma so severe that even his vaunted healing powers cannot overcome the psychological scars that define his character.

Windsor-Smith leaned into influences from Art Nouveau, Pre-Raphaelites, and cyberpunk to create an origin story worthy of Marvel's most popular character—an antihero killer that proved the Comics Code Authority was a relic of the past.

In telling Wolverine's origin, Windsor-Smith did not just rely on the popularity of the character to create a popular book; he used complex storytelling techniques, blended with R-rated levels of graphic violence, and stunning, almost painterly color art. The results are one of Marvel's strangest comics, and also a perennial seller in Marvel's library that has been reprinted and enjoyed by several generations of fans ever since it appeared in 1991.

In the history of American comic books, very few have achieved the status of perennial sellers—*Dark Knight Returns*, *Maus*, *Batman: Year One*, *Watchmen*, *Sandman*, *Understanding Comics*, *Teenage Mutant Ninja Turtles*, *Walking Dead*, *Smile*, and *Bone*. Despite artists and writers striving to create new and original stories, these efforts rarely connect with a wide audience and when they do, they often fade over time. *Weapon X* is a unicorn because it defies this pattern. It was celebrated in its day and continues to thrill new fans 35 years later. To understand its success, we will strip *Weapon X* like Barry Windsor-Smith stripped Wolverine and we will examine its form and content to better understand the phenomenon that is *Weapon X*.

2

Wolverine 1991

Who Is Wolverine?

Wolverine is a short, hairy loner with a shorter temper, antisocial tendencies, a weird haircut, and the mantra, "I'm the best there is at what I do." Although it is never stated explicitly, violence is what he does. His bones are reinforced with adamantium, the strongest metal in the Marvel Universe. Imagine an Irish kiss with that forehead. He also has six long claws that are made of adamantium and can cut through anything. He studied martial arts extensively and claims that his fighting prowess is such that there is no difference between his actions and thoughts. This is useful when a psychic opponent can read his thoughts. Because his thoughts and actions are one, Wolverine can overcome this kind of threat. He possesses certain animalistic characteristics, specifically his sense of smell. He never forgets a person's scent and can track them

60¢
1
SEPT
A MARVEL COMICS LIMITED SERIES
WOLVERINE

MARVEL
AT LAST— IN HIS OWN MONTHLY SERIES!
WOLVERINE
$1.50 US
1
NOV

MARVEL
WOLVERINE
$1.50 US
17
LATE NOV

40¢
133
MAY
MARVEL COMICS GROUP
THE UNCANNY
X-MEN
ALL OF THE X-MEN HAVE FALLEN BEFORE THE MIGHT OF THE HELLFIRE CLUB--ALL EXCEPT ONE!
WOLVERINE LASHES OUT!
50¢
MARVEL COMICS GROUP
THE UNCANNY
X-MEN
SLAIN
APPREHENDED
CYCLOPS
COLOSSUS
STORM
NIGHTCRAWLER
ANGEL
ICEMAN
BEAST
SPRITE
WOLVERINE
ATTENTION!
YOU ARE NOW LEAVING A

MARVEL
25th
ANNIVERSARY
THE UNCANNY
X-MEN
75¢
207
JULY

MARVEL
25th
ANNIVERSARY
THE UNCANNY
X-MEN
WOLVERINE VS. SABRETOOTH-- ROUND 1!
75¢ US
212 DEC

MARVEL
25th
ANNIVERSARY
CLASSIC
X-MEN
$1.00 US
$1.25 CAN
1 SEP

through crowds from quite a distance. He also moves with the stealth of the ninja. He demonstrates this stealth by sneaking up on deer and touching them before they realize he is near. His mutant power is a healing ability, so he is practically immortal. This is a bit of a double-edged sword because he frequently endures punishment, devastating injuries, and excruciating pain that would kill anyone else. His real name is Logan. He is Canadian.

That is pretty much everything that was known about Wolverine when *Weapon X* was published in 1991.

Wolverine made his first full appearance in *The Incredible Hulk* 181 (November 1974, writer: Len Wein, artist: Herb Trimpe, editor: Roy Thomas, character design: John Romita), as a special agent of the Canadian government. As first appearances and debuts go, this one is awesome. The character goes toe-to-toe with an enraged Hulk. Although he ultimately fails to stop the Hulk, he gives the powerhouse a good fight. And fans responded very positively to this new character. In *The Incredible Hulk* 184 letter column, the editor wrote:

> Reader feedback on issue #181 has been *pouring* in, and the collective judgment of Hulkdom is an instantaneous and unanimous acclaim for the wondrous Wolverine. We're not sure whether it's his charisma as a character, or his Canadian

INCREDIBLE HULK
MARVEL COMICS GROUP TM
APPROVED BY THE COMICS CODE AUTHORITY
25¢ 181 NOV 02456
THE INCREDIBLE HULK TM
HE'S HERE! THE WORLD'S FIRST AND GREATEST CANADIAN SUPER-HERO!
AND NOW... the WOLVERINE!
AND THE SURVIVOR OF THEIR EPIC BATTLE MUST FACE-- the WENDIGO!

origin, but whatever it is—whew! You may be sure that we have plans for the Wolverine, so keep your eyes peeled…

Dean Mullaney wrote a fan letter praising the character. Mullaney would go on to become founder and publisher of Eclipse Comics, one of the most successful American comic book publishers of the 1980s.

Wolverine's first appearance as a cameo was actually in the last panel of *Incredible Hulk* 180. And in that panel, there is a reference to Weapon X. Earlier in the issue, the Canadian military discovers that the Hulk has returned to Canada. After the destruction of his previous visit, the authorities decide to send Weapon X after him!

The Incredible Hulk 181 did not just feature Wolverine's first full appearance, it also gave more background on Weapon X. As Canadian military officials observe Wolverine's efforts to subdue the Hulk, these officials refer to Wolverine as "Weapon X."

Their description of the character is consistent with Windsor-Smith's *Weapon X* story, "the government has spent a great deal of time, effort, and money, developing that mutant's natural-born speed, strength and ***savagery*** [emphasis mine] into the skills of a professional warrior and despite the few kinks that still remain in his psychological makeup, I think we've done a pretty good job!" This panel becomes much darker after reading

Weapon X and seeing exactly how the military developed Wolverine's skills.

The following year, Wolverine joined the X-Men in *Giant-Size X-Men* 1. Writer Chris Claremont spent the next fifteen years writing *X-Men* and developing the Wolverine character. During that time, *The Uncanny X-Men* became Marvel's best-selling title and Wolverine became the most popular X-Men.

To understand Wolverine's popularity, it may be helpful to consider comics history. For their first 50–60 years, comic books were commercial entertainment. Their primary distribution model was through news-stands. In the late 1970s, a new distribution model emerged. People began selling comic books through specialty stores known as comic shops. To support this new sales outlet, the distribution expanded from news-stand distribution to include the "direct market" distribution. In the direct market, comic book dealers arranged to buy non-returnable comics from the publishers at a deeper discount than news-stands. Since the books were non-returnable, each copy sold to a comic book store was final regardless of whether the comic book store sold the book to a consumer or not. News-stands on the other hand returned unsold copies or more accurately, ripped off the covers and returned those to the publishers as proof of "unsold" copies, only paying for the copies that the news-stand sold. This was a very inefficient model. The direct market also meant that

GIANT-SIZE X-MEN
68 BIG PAGES
MARVEL COMICS GROUP
APPROVED BY THE COMICS CODE AUTHORITY
1
1975
02940
50¢
GIANT-SIZE
X-MEN
SENSES-SHATTERING 1ST ISSUE!
NEW!
DEADLY GENESIS!
GK DEC

stores and distributors began ordering books before they were printed. Preorders allowed publishers greater accuracy to set their print runs. This accuracy led to less waste in the form of over-printing and unsold copies, and thus more profit. Soon publishers began to experiment with different types of comics because this new distribution model changed the business model dramatically. It allowed publishers and creators to sell fewer comic books and make more money due to greater efficiency.

The direct market opened the door to books that weren't designed for the widest audience possible, or the lowest common denominators. Creators and publishers could create content that was more personal, esoteric, or experimental because they could reach readers, or at least buyers, directly. Another big change was the influence of the Comics Code Authority. Their authority was limited to news-stand distribution and sales. Comic book stores did not use news-stand distributors and therefore did not require the Comics Code. This allowed publishers to make comics aimed at adult readers. In the past, young readers would outgrow comic books. But with more mature comics, publishers could extend their target demographic to include older readers. Antiheroes and super hero characters with more ambiguous moral codes began to rise in popularity. Fans voted with their wallets and super heroes grew darker and more violent. It should be noted that violent crime also rose in the 1970s and 1980s, as did the threat of nuclear war and tensions in the Cold War and in the Middle East. Although it is impossible to say exactly why super heroes' values changed, it is probably some combination of society, media, new business models, and an aging consumer base that contributed to these changes. Characters like Superman and Spider-Man faced competition from new outlaw "heroes" like the Punisher, Lobo, and Ghost Rider. The most popular member of these new violent characters was Wolverine. He was the right character at the right time—no-nonsense, dangerous, mysterious, and cool. Fans loved him, even if some parents did not.

By 1991, Wolverine rivaled Spider-Man as Marvel's most popular character. He starred in his own comic book series, *Wolverine*. He appeared in *Uncanny X-Men*, *Classic X-Men*, and the bi-weekly *Marvel Comics Presents*. He was a member of the "new" Fantastic Four and appeared in special editions and mini-series.

In the summer of 1991, Marvel launched a second, ongoing *X-Men* comic book to complement *Uncanny X-Men*. The first issue of the new *X-Men* comic sold a record eight million copies. On the cover, Wolverine is front and center of the team with fangs bared and claws out, ready to do what he really did best in 1991—sell comic books.

The other important thing about Wolverine at this time is

MARVEL COMICS
1ST ISSUE! A LEGEND REBORN!
X-MEN
A MUTANT MILE-STONE!
© 1991 MARVEL ENT. GROUP, INC.
$1.50 US
$1.80 CAN/UK 80p
1
OCT
01772
APPROVED BY THE COMICS CODE AUTHORITY
JIM SCOTT

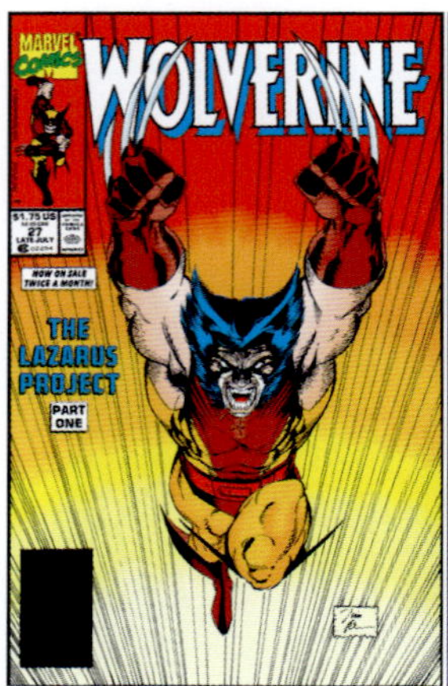
MARVEL COMICS
WOLVERINE
$1.75 US
27
LATE JULY
NOW ON SALE TWICE A MONTH!
THE LAZARUS PROJECT
PART ONE

MARVEL
THE UNCANNY
X-MEN
$1.00 US
251
EARLY NOV
NOW ON SALE TWICE A MONTH!

MARVEL
THE INCREDIBLE
HULK
75¢ US
340
FEB

MARVEL
THE PUNISHER
war journal
GUEST-STARRING WOLVERINE
$1.50 US
6
JUN
SAGA!
MEETING FOR THE FIRST TIME-- AND MAYBE THE LAST!
MARVEL COMICS
THE NEW MUTANTS
$1.00 US
93
SEPT
YOU KNEW IT HAD TO HAPPEN! CABLE VERSUS WOLVERINE! ALL THIS-- AND SUNFIRE, TOO!!

MARVEL COMICS
THE WORLD'S MOST COMMERCIALEST COMIC MAGAZINE!
Fantastic Four
$1.00 US
348
JAN
GHOST RIDER! HULK! WOLVERINE! AND SPIDER-MAN!

WOLVERINE
the jungle adventure
walter SIMONSON
michael MIGNOLA
bob WIACEK

A WOLVERINE Gallery

that his origin was completely unknown, even to him. In super hero comics, origin stories are integral to the hero. They often define the character and his or her mission. Somehow, Marvel had turned Wolverine into one of the most popular super hero characters in the world without telling anyone his origin. By 1991, Wolverine starred in a half-dozen monthly comics, plus one-shots, specials, reprints, and annuals, and no one knew how he became the best at what he did or why he did what he did. All they knew is that they liked him.

Because Marvel had not given its readers much info about Wolverine's past, fans were hungry to learn more. They wrote letters speculating and asking questions about his background. While some fans desperately wanted answers, others worried that revealing Wolverine's past could ruin the character. After all, part of his appeal was the mystery surrounding him.

So when Marvel announced *Weapon X*, Wolverine's origin, it was a big deal! After fifteen years, readers were finally going to learn Wolverine's secrets. Or at least we thought we were going to learn his secrets…

3

Cast of Characters

The cast of *Weapon X* is small. Logan, the Professor, Dr. Abraham Cornelius, and Miss Carol Hines are the main characters. Beyond those four, there are henchmen or guards, young technicians that assist with the experiment, and animals that serve as field tests for Weapon X. There is one more mysterious character who interacts with the Professor over some kind of audio communication device, but they never appear in a panel.

Logan, a.k.a. Wolverine, a.k.a. Weapon X, is discussed in the previous chapter so the focus of this chapter is on the rest of the cast.

Miss Carol Hines comes from NASA. She is a computer expert. She sets up equipment and monitors Weapon X, the drugs, the adamantium process, etc. She is a supporting character in the story. Unlike Dr. Cornelius who faces criminal charges for his past and views Experiment-X as a

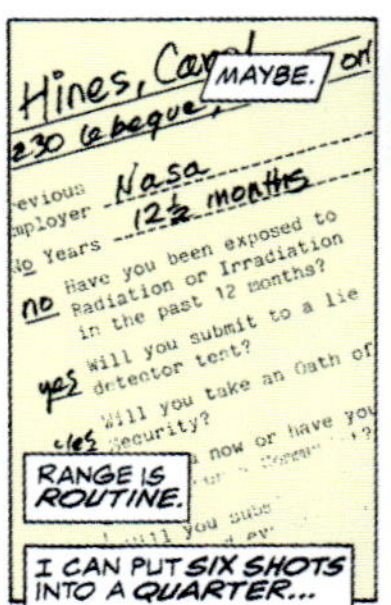

lifeline, it is not clear why Hines joins Experiment-X. Perhaps it is just a well-paid job for her robust computer skillset. After all, the 1960s setting was not known as a time when women had a lot of opportunities in computer science. Hines expresses sympathy for Logan a few times in the story as well as reservations about the project but she never acts on them.

When Weapon X breaks free of his controllers, the Professor uses Hines to lure Weapon X into a trap. The Professor planned to sacrifice Hines as bait, but Weapon X spared her life. Should readers view Hines as innocent or sympathetic? She is certainly more likable than the Professor, but her actions do not support this view. She agrees to support Dr. Cornelius when he grows wary of the experiment, but it is not Hines that initiates this momentary and ineffectual act of conscience. Her role in the story is not clear. Why did Experiment-X or, more accurately, why did Windsor-Smith choose her?

Hines is the only woman in the story. In the prologue,

Logan thinks about his mother, a woman he does not know or remember. There is no other mention of a woman in the story. When Hines does become a factor, she is used as a damsel in distress to try to lure Weapon X into a trap—a rather traditional gender role in the super hero genre and the men's adventure or action genre. Despite her obvious ability with technology, she does not have a title like Dr. Cornelius or the Professor. She is the most mysterious or perhaps the least developed character in the story. Nothing of significance is revealed about her over the course of this story.

With her background in computer science, she is responsible for making Weapon X a remote-controlled killer. Cornelius is not a programmer, he is a physician. So perhaps her role is more significant but it is not detailed in the story.

Dr. Abraham Cornelius comes from the wrong side of

the law. He is an American doctor wanted for murder. Police files and newspaper headlines in the prologue reveal that his crime is physician-assisted suicide like Dr. Kevorkian. The Professor needs a physician to keep Logan alive throughout Experiment-X. The choice of Dr. Cornelius suggests that the Professor and Experiment-X are shady. They even meet on a dark street corner compared with the more traditional office setting for the meeting between Hines and the Professor.

Dr. Cornelius works closely with Hines. Both monitor the progress of various medical procedures as well as the tests and field trials that Weapon X endures. Cornelius seems to be the character that is most uncomfortable with or at least most vocal

about his unease over Experiment-X. That makes sense since it contradicts the Hippocratic oath that medical professionals take.

Another interesting thing about Dr. Cornelius is his resemblance to one of Wolverine's most celebrated artists—John Byrne. Byrne was one of the most popular comic book creators at Marvel and DC Comics in the 1980s. His star was built on *Uncanny X-Men*, a title he drew from issue 108 (1977) to issue 143 (1981). There is a well-known story that Chris Claremont, the writer of *Uncanny X-Men* from 1975–1991, was going to kill the character of Wolverine. John Byrne objected. Both Byrne and Wolverine are Canadian, so Byrne did not want the book's only Canadian character to die. Byrne served the same role in real life that Dr. Cornelius serves in Weapon X. Was this a clever Easter Egg by Windsor-Smith or merely coincidence? Either way, the character design bears an unusually strong resemblance to the famous X-Men artist.

Speaking of visual coincidences, the Professor looks a lot like Charles Xavier, a.k.a. Professor X, the founder of the X-Men.

> "There's one main boss," Windsor-Smith relates. "He's called the Professor, oddly enough. And he looks like bloody Professor X, which is weird. Nobody pointed this out to me! I had done 10 stories and I'm thinking, 'Who does this guy

look like? He's sort of tall and he's bald and he wears glasses.' He looks just like Professor X!"

In case there are any lingering doubts, Windsor-Smith is quick to put them down.

"He's not," he says flatly. "It's total coincidence. And he doesn't have a name, like Professor Jones. He's just a very neurotic, amoral, manipulating son-of-a-bitch." (*Comics Scene* 18, April 1991, pp. 23–24)

Although both characters have bald heads and serious demeanors, they do not share the same attitude about mutants.

Like most characters in *Weapon X*, the description of the Professor is minimal. His appearances are all contained within the Experiment-X facility. It is not clear what kind of person he is when he is not at work. He appears insecure. Weapon X attempts to harm him early in the story. It is why he is willing to destroy Weapon X later in the story. There is also an event when the Professor first attempts to control Weapon X. The interface is sensitive. The Professor struggles with it and causes awkward, jerky movements of Weapon X, eliciting laughter from the lab technicians. The Professor explodes with anger at Cornelius and the lab techs over their reaction. He hates being mocked and ridiculed by them.

The Professor appears to be Weapon X's architect as well as the story's primary antagonist. However, a few scenes feature the Professor communicating with someone in a higher position of power.

This off-panel presence was a compromise. According to the *Comics Scene* 18 interview with Windsor-Smith, when Chris Claremont learned about *Weapon X*, he was not happy.

> "We never quite see who the main mover is in this series. There is another force at work. He's never seen, you never hear him. I never explain who he is. There are clues as to who it might be. This is the only thing about the series that really isn't mine."

In his enthusiasm for the *Weapon X* project, Windsor-Smith overlooked the writer who is most closely identified with the feral X-Man, and an accommodation had to be reached over the villain.

"I really wasn't thinking about Chris Claremont a whole lot. It didn't occur to me that he might have an idea about Logan's origin. I guess what was in the back of my mind was that if Chris did have an idea, he would have done it before now. I thought this was a clean avenue. So, when I took the first two stories down, Chris was a little upset. He didn't make that too apparent to me, but I've heard since that he was upset that I had encroached on his territory. Chris had a specific person whom he was going to, in the far future, have tell the story of how Logan became Wolverine, and this person did it to him." (*Comics Scene* 18, April 1991, p. 23)

Claremont stopped writing *X-Men* in late 1991 with *X-Men* (1991) issue 3. Since then, Marvel has published a lot of information about Wolverine's origin as well as several series and stories about Weapon X. The original plan that Claremont had for Wolverine's origin seems to have changed completely. With that said, it is fun to consider who Claremont planned to reveal as the person behind Wolverine's origin.

The biggest clue I found in *Weapon X* is in the center of page 4 of the story's prologue. "Apocalypse" is written in bold

SPENDIN' MY NIGHTS AT THE PROPHECY...

IT'S FOR FALLEN CHRISTIANS, Y'KNOW.

I AIN'T GOT THAT STUFF, BUT I LIED TO GET THROUGH THE DOOR.

HEY, IT'S FREE.

FOR TH' FALLEN.

SO...

...I GUESS I QUALIFY.

PROPHECY IS PART OF THE APOCALYPSE.

DIDJA KNOW THAT?

I DIDN'T.

SOME DRUNK BUM DOWN THE HALL TOLD ME THAT.

SPAT AS HE SAID IT, TOO.

THEN HE CROAKED.

HAPPENS A LOT 'ROUND HERE.

BEEN THINKIN 'BOUT MOVIN' ON.

font. Remember, this was not the first story or installment that Windsor-Smith created for *Weapon X*. The chapters were written and drawn out of sequence.

Apocalypse is a supervillain in the X-Men Universe. He is the first mutant. His first appearance came in *X-Factor* 5 (1986). He operated behind the scenes as the leader of the Alliance of Evil. In subsequent appearances, he transformed Angel into Archangel and the Hulk into War, one of the Four Horsemen of the Apocalypse.

Apocalypse is known for transforming characters into more dangerous, darker versions of themselves. In *Wolverine: Jungle Adventure*, Wolverine finds an adamantium skull in one of Apocalypse's labs.

The identity of the character behind Windsor-Smith's *Weapon X* may be unknown or irrelevant based on the subsequent 35 years of continuity but it is another footnote to this strange origin.

Regardless of their identity, the Professor's paranoia extends to his superior. As Weapon X breaks free, the Professor realizes that the mysterious entity behind the experiment may consider the Professor expendable along with the rest of the staff. When the project breaks down, the Professor throws Cornelius and Hines at Weapon X to save himself. Was he part of Operation Paperclip? Perhaps his paranoia is one more Cold War detail that Windsor-Smith includes in this tale.

In the end, his actions paint him as a coward and a bigot. With the revelation that he is not the mastermind behind Experiment-X, even his intellectual mad scientist identity is marred. He is little more than a pawn in Wolverine's origin.

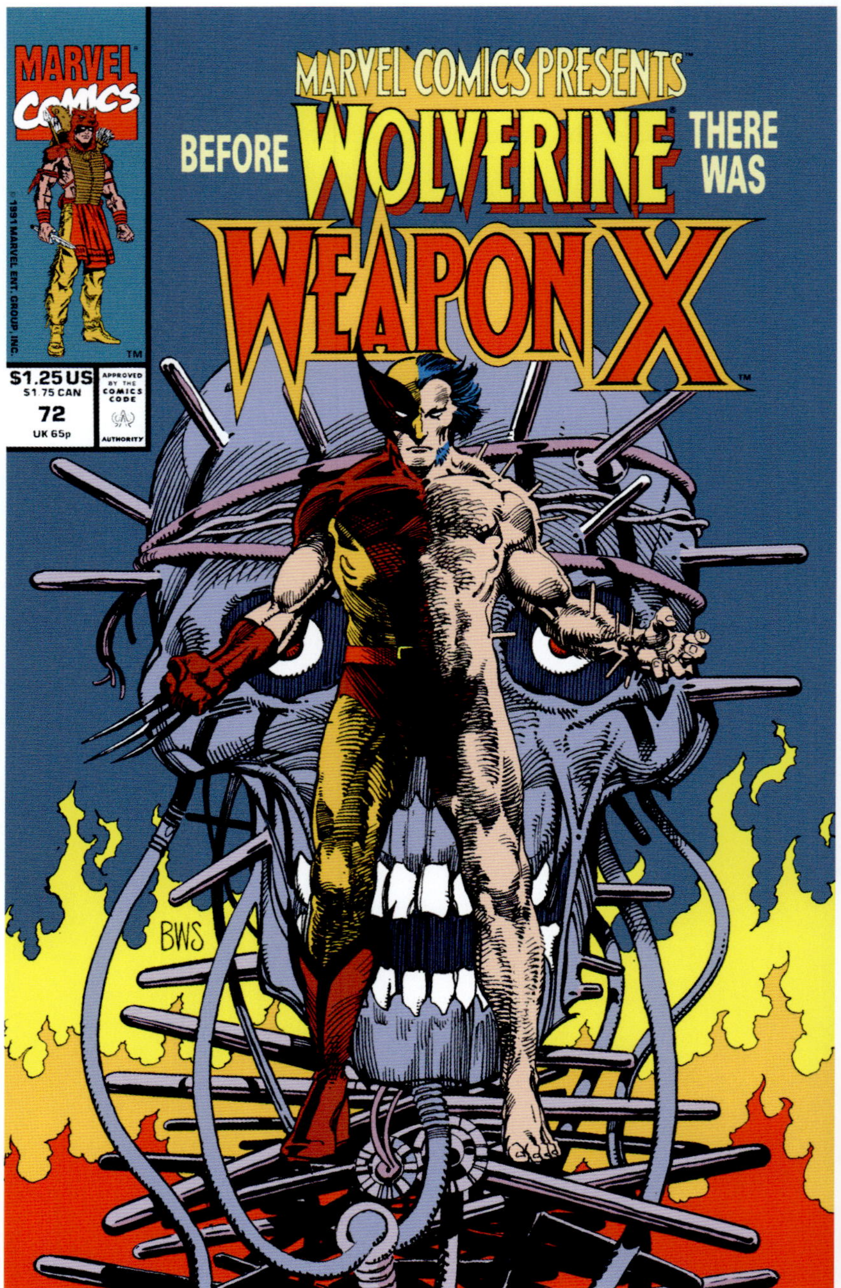
MARVEL COMICS
MARVEL COMICS PRESENTS
BEFORE WOLVERINE THERE WAS
WEAPON X
$1.25 US
$1.75 CAN
72
UK 65p
APPROVED BY THE COMICS CODE AUTHORITY
©1991 MARVEL ENT. GROUP, INC.
BWS

4

Weapon X: Story

Weapon X…Prologue

When the first installment of *Weapon X* hit the news-stands. I anticipated it eagerly!

The cover of *Marvel Comics Presents* 72 sets the tone perfectly for the Weapon X story. There is a full figure of Wolverine. Half of the figure is the orange and brown costume he wore in the 1980s and the other half of the figure is naked. Behind the figure is a skull with metal prongs and wires protruding. Eyeballs stare out of the hollow sockets in the skull and somehow without the aid of eyebrows or other facial features, Windsor-Smith is able to make the eyes expressive. Their expression is one of fear. Behind everything are flames. No doubt the flames of hell that will forge the perfect killing machine. I redrew this cover in my sketchbook as soon as I got home!

The text on the cover said it all—"Before Wolverine, there was Weapon X."

The inside cover featured the table of contents for this anthology series.

WEAPON-X

Prologue

A 13 Part Story

"Long before the X-Men, before even Wolverine…there is simply Logan, the mutant."

By: BARRY WINDSOR-SMITH

Letterer – JIM NOVAK and BARRY WINDSOR-SMITH

The three other stories were all created by teams of at least five people. It is rare to have a single person handling the whole process.

On rereading, the first thing I note is the thirteen-part story. It calls to mind the iconic *Friday the 13th* horror franchise. This story is more horror than super hero after all, and in another world, Weapon X and/or Wolverine would make a fantastic design for an Eighties horror slasher.

The first installment is not part one, but rather a prologue that sets up the cast. The opening panels cleverly turn "Experiment-X" into "X-Men" through the Professor's glasses via Windsor-Smith's composition. The Professor is the first character we see. He puts on his glasses and we (or he) see a

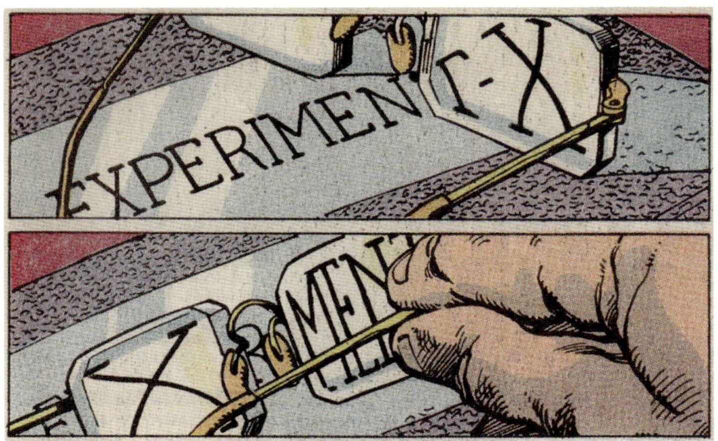

close-up of Logan's forlorn face. Despite Windsor-Smith's claim of pure coincidence, it is hard not to see Professor X in the Professor's character design.

The prologue establishes the Professor as the architect behind the Experiment-X program, or at least he appears to be the architect behind the program as he assembles the pieces and people who populate the story.

Panel 4 cuts to Logan. Caption boxes reveal his inner monologue. These first eight pages are the only part of Weapon X that reveal any inner thoughts from Logan. After the prologue, that inner monologue disappears. Through captions, we learn that Logan senses a storm is coming. The "big one." He imagines writing a letter home to his "goat-headed…witch" of a mother. Then he admits that he doesn't know who his mother was. His past is a mystery to readers and to the character himself.

The use of text is unusual in this prologue. Besides Logan's interior narration, a lot of text appears in the illustrations within the panels. There are pages from files, newspaper headlines and clippings, text on computer screens, and handwriting on forms. The use of text in the art reveals information about the characters: The Professor has a file an inch thick for Experiment-X; Dr. Cornelius is a fugitive medical doctor on the run; Carol Hines worked for NASA for a year; and Logan is concerned over the mounting public hysteria against mutants.

There is no dialogue in the prologue. This contrasts with the rest of the story where the Professor's, Cornelius', and Hines' dialogue makes up the bulk of the story's text. But it fits with and establishes the overall storytelling style of *Weapon X*. The selective use of text requires the reader to study the art closely in order to understand what is happening. This division between text and image contrasts dramatically with the standard Marvel method that Stan Lee popularized at the dawn of the Marvel Universe (in the 1960s). The traditional Marvel style relied on captions and expositional dialogue that often reiterated what the visuals illustrated. It could be described as "show *and* tell." This was an effective method of clear communication when the audience's average age was 7. However, *Weapon X* is not aimed at 7-year-olds, and the complexity of Windsor-Smith's storytelling reflects this. Although the specific format of text changes with chapter one, the density of text and illustration is consistent between the prologue and subsequent chapters. If the reader is not focused on each panel of *Weapon X*, they will miss some of the information that Windsor-Smith provides.

As the prologue's eight pages unfold, panels cut between Logan and the Professor. This cross cutting between the two main characters begins on page one. This technique of cutting between settings and time from panel to panel will continue throughout the installment. It is a technique that will appear in other chapters as well. In the prologue, it allows the reader to follow different characters as they move towards an intersection point in chapter one. In future chapters, the use of temporal and spatial cuts distorts reality or disrupts the perception of the reader and the characters for narrative purposes.

The Professor spends the prologue setting up Experiment-X. He hires Dr. Cornelius, who is on the run because he assisted patients in suicide. Cornelius' specialty is drugs and using drugs not just to kill people but also to keep them alive. That will be his primary responsibility with Logan—drugging him and ensuring that he survives the brutal "experiments" that lie ahead. Next the Professor hires Carol Hines to set up and run the computer equipment in the lab. That equipment will control and monitor the experiment under the direction of Dr. Cornelius and the Professor. Linking Hines to NASA is an interesting choice. By the late 1980s, some conspiracy theorists challenged NASA's integrity and the validity of the moon landing. Is this NASA reference a nod to conspiracy theories or an inconsequential detail? *Weapon X* contains several conspiracy theory references to things like MK-Ultra and human experimentation, so it is not unreasonable to consider NASA's inclusion as part of a theme of government mistrust. This story is filled with questions and secrets.

As the pieces of the Experiment-X program come together, documents reveal that Logan is/was a member of the military, police, or intelligence, and that he was involved in a fatal accident at the gun range. He "wing[ed] some geek with a ricochet…" The "geek" was critically wounded. The document describes Logan as self-destructive, having a nervous disorder or psychosis, and suffering from chronic alcohol abuse. The document advises that "immediate dismissal is imperative." Logan is not likable, heroic, or particularly sympathetic in *Weapon X*. Psychologically, Logan is an antihero in a dark place. If this story stood on its own, without the weight of Logan's Wolverine adventures, readers might view this story much differently. While the events are horrific, Windsor-Smith does not offer any redeeming qualities concerning the title character. Kind of refreshing. Again, unlike most Marvel comics.

During his suspension or more likely after his dismissal, Logan spends time in a hotel for fallen Christians called the Prophecy. “Prophecy is part of the apocalypse. Didja know that?” Logan’s narration reveals that he ain’t got that Christian stuff but he’s definitely fallen. Judging by Logan’s room, the hotel looks like it has fallen on hard times itself. A large panel features a close-up of Logan’s bloody hand next to a bottle of Canadian whisky, a snub-nosed .38 revolver, and pills. The newspaper headline proclaims, “Outcry Over Mutants!” The long shot reveals Logan passed out on a couch in a rundown, one-room unit. A sink stands in the corner.

The prologue also features a couple of panels that suggest things to come, like Logan in restraints and being wrangled by armed men. He suffers from nightmares, dreams of death, shadowy rooms, pain, spikes, and daggers hands! “With… Vile…stench…and…horror.”

There are panels of experiments with monkeys—experiments that will be conducted on Logan. The temporal structure of *Weapon X* is another unique element of its storytelling and it starts in this prologue. The cuts between panels are not just spatial as the narrative shows us Logan and the Professor before their paths intersect. The cuts also jump forward and backward in time. Flashbacks. Foreshadowing. Memories—real or fake, it’s impossible to tell. Seeing these moments out of sequence is haunting. How does one represent trauma in a super hero comic book? Knowing what unfolds in this story adds a weight to these images. It feels like they are traumatic experiences that Logan will carry with him forever. And maybe that trauma is so severe that ripples extend into the past. Does Logan sense what is about to happen to him?

Some people believe that traumatic, intense events can echo forward and backward through time. These panels suggest that effect. The legendary film editor Walter Murch wrote extensively on his editing theories. One idea he had was to cut out the climactic moment of the scene when the scene was not working. This left a void of anticipation and reverberation that relied on the audience to fill with their imagination. A practical example of this can be seen in horror movies, specifically slasher movies, when violence is implied but not explicitly shown on screen. Through clever editing, the actual killing moments can be transposed into the audience's mind, often resulting in a greater emotional impact than if it were shown clearly on screen. One may also interpret these time-displaced panels as fate, destiny, or God's Will (especially considering that Logan is staying at the Prophecy and talking about Christianity). In other words, *Weapon X* and its events were always a part of Logan. Even if the events do not take place until now, their inevitability defies the linear, conventional timeline.

While the idea or a theme of time manipulation may sound far-fetched, there will be additional, compelling examples of this in later chapters of *Weapon X*. And it may be worth noting now that Windsor-Smith wrote and drew *Weapon X* out of sequence. As a subsequent Windsor-Smith project, *Unity* (1992, Valiant Comics), explained—time is not absolute.

Visually, the prologue is dense. There are 59 panels on these 8 pages, more than 6 per page on average. The panels feature many close-ups and tightly cropped compositions. There is a lot of text on these pages including sound effects, narrative captions, and illustrated text in images. The information density exceeds the average Marvel comic of 1991. The format of *Marvel Comics Presents*, 8-page stories or chapters, necessitates a different pace than a typical Marvel comic book from 1991 that has 20–22 story pages. However, other stories in *Marvel Comics Present*s do not feature this level of density. Windsor-Smith may have been responding to the eight-page format of the book but interviews suggest he also wanted to tell the story in a way that was different from the typical Stan Lee/Chris Claremont/Marvel method approach. In an interview with *Wizard* magazine (issue 28, p. 84), he describes his initial intent. "I originally intended to do about five issues of obscure storytelling with very flashy graphics. It was just something I fancied doing, not getting into a long storyline. I just wanted to do something that would be more graphics-oriented…"

Although Logan and the Experiment-X team do not meet in this prologue, a strong sense of dread and foreboding permeates these pages. Logan in particular seems sick, like someone bottoming out. Indeed, Logan's condition will be referenced later in the story by the Professor as he attempts to justify the inhumane Experiment-X.

This opening installment makes clear that *Weapon X* is not a children's story. It establishes horror, not super hero, as its primary genre.

The use of color as a storytelling device will be the subject of examination later in this volume but it should be acknowledged here. Windsor-Smith uses color in a couple of ways. One is informational, where different color text boxes indicate different speakers. It is also used aesthetically, where color establishes mood, tone, and setting. Color is integral to the information density in *Weapon X*.

On the last page of the prologue, there are six panels. Five of the panels focus on Logan as he looks through a rainy window into the stormy, night sky. Lightning strikes the Prophecy's sign and Logan's narration exclaims that "…Hell is comin'." The panel that does not focus on Logan is a pile of tubes, intravenous needles, and blood. Text on the bottom of the page states, "Weapon-X begins in two weeks…" But the panel of bloody medical equipment contradicts this text. *Weapon X* has already begun. It began before Wolverine entered the Marvel Universe in *Incredible Hulk* 181. The trauma of *Weapon X* is always.

Weapon X…Chapter One

> "Logan has been taken captive by a group of mysterious men."

The cover is an image of Logan suspended in a green liquid. Unconscious. Bubbles disturb the liquid around his figure. His hair is long. Dozens of metal rods protrude from his body as well as a few wires or tubes.

This chapter continues to cross-cut between two different settings and time. The common element is Logan.

There are five panels on page one. Four depict Logan's capture and one panel shows Logan, unconscious, shaved, and naked with wires and a breathing apparatus connected to his mouth. He is in a tank that is filling with a red liquid. The cross cutting here illustrates the inevitability of Logan's fate. We see him struggle against his abductors, but we also know how that turns out. Time is not linear in Weapon X.

MARVEL COMICS
MARVEL COMICS PRESENTS
WEAPON X
© 1991 MARVEL ENT. GROUP, INC.
$1.25 US
$1.75 CAN
73
CC 02214
APPROVED BY THE COMICS CODE AUTHORITY
BWS

Physical force was necessary to subdue Logan. His abductors pistol-whipped him to knock him out. As this first administration of adamantium is applied to Logan, the team discovers that the wounds from his abduction are completely healed. His hair also grows back in the course of about twenty minutes—the duration of the experimental process depicted on this cover. Hines notes that Logan's medical record indicates that he has been shot five times. However, scans of his body show no scars or other indications of these wounds. Logan also requires more drugs throughout this process and absorbs more adamantium than expected. Dr. Cornelius notes that Logan's reaction is unprecedented and suggests that he is "more than human." We know that he is a mutant, but it appears that this is news to the team, including the Professor. With this information, the Professor walks out in the middle of the experiment or, as Cornelius calls it, the "middle of a crisis."

At the beginning of chapter one the color blue prevails. Logan's captors surround him outside a bar at night. As the chapter progresses, the pages transition to more and more red as the story moves from abduction to laboratory, from nature to artificial. The final page is almost completely red. The team has stabilized their test subject and the process has taught them more about Logan's resilience.

Another interesting note on the color in chapter one—the main color is red, but the cover of *Marvel Comics Presents*

73 is dominated by its complementary color, green—like undigested bile.

Weapon X...Chapter Two

> "The Professor has begun his mysterious experiment on Logan."

Two big revelations occur in chapter two.

First, the Professor consults an unseen superior over the revelation that Logan is a mutant. His unseen master knew that Logan was a mutant. With this "super human power to regenerate damaged tissue," the Professor observes that Logan "could be just about immortal!" He asks his boss, "what else do I not know about Experiment X?"

Chapter Two is the first clear indication of an influential presence above the Professor in the Experiment-X program. That character's identity will remain shrouded in mystery during Weapon X. There is no closure. When Weapon X ends, the audience has more questions than answers. This open ending is another non-traditional storytelling choice by Windsor-Smith.

Chapter two continues to cross-cut between different spaces. The first part of Logan's treatment continues while the Professor questions the unknown character responsible

MARVEL COMICS
MARVEL COMICS PRESENTS
WEAPON X
$1.25 US
$1.75 CAN
74
02214
APPROVED BY THE COMICS CODE AUTHORITY
© 1991 MARVEL ENT. GROUP, INC.

for this project. During this initial exposure to adamantium, another surprise occurs when excess metal collects in Logan's forearms.

This chapter concludes the experimental procedure as well as the aftermath of the procedure. At first, Logan is unconscious and under observation in Laboratory 2. Slowly, he begins to stir. He stares at his hands. They start bleeding. Then claws cut through the skin on the back of Logan's hands! Everyone reacts with surprise, including Logan.

His body starts to thrash. He doesn't speak; he may not be capable of speech. He has endured a major medical experiment that involved bonding metal with his bones. Bloody claws have torn through his flesh and wires and probes protrude from his naked body.

He is in a room with strange light patterns that resemble a background from *2001: A Space Odyssey*. If that is intentional, it is worth noting the connection between Stanley Kubrick, NASA, and the moon landing in conspiracy lore. The lab looks like a 1970s sci-fi movie set. The gridded, saturated colors and hard lines contrast graphically against Logan's pink, fleshy body and organic lines. Graphically, this is pure cyberpunk—they are building a mutant cyborg.

The Professor orders an inexperienced, unarmed lab-worker to enter Logan's room to "try to help the poor man!" While the Professor watches the monitor, Dr. Cornelius grabs a couple of security guys and heads to Laboratory 2 to see what is happening.

When Cornelius arrives, the lab-worker is dead! Disemboweled.

Logan's claws are covered in blood. He stands over the murdered boy "like a mad animal!"

The Professor observes the murder through the monitor and succinctly describes it with one disturbing word.

Weapon X…Chapter Three

"While the Professor questioned his mysterious leader about Logan's mutant, Weapon X manifested his claws…"

After murdering the lab boy, Logan crashes through the observation window towards Dr. Cornelius. Before he can strike, he collapses, having torn away his life-support.

Understandably, Cornelius is shaken and in a raw emotional state. "I've helped you create a monster," he tells the Professor.

"Yes. But we can make him behave!" the Professor replies.

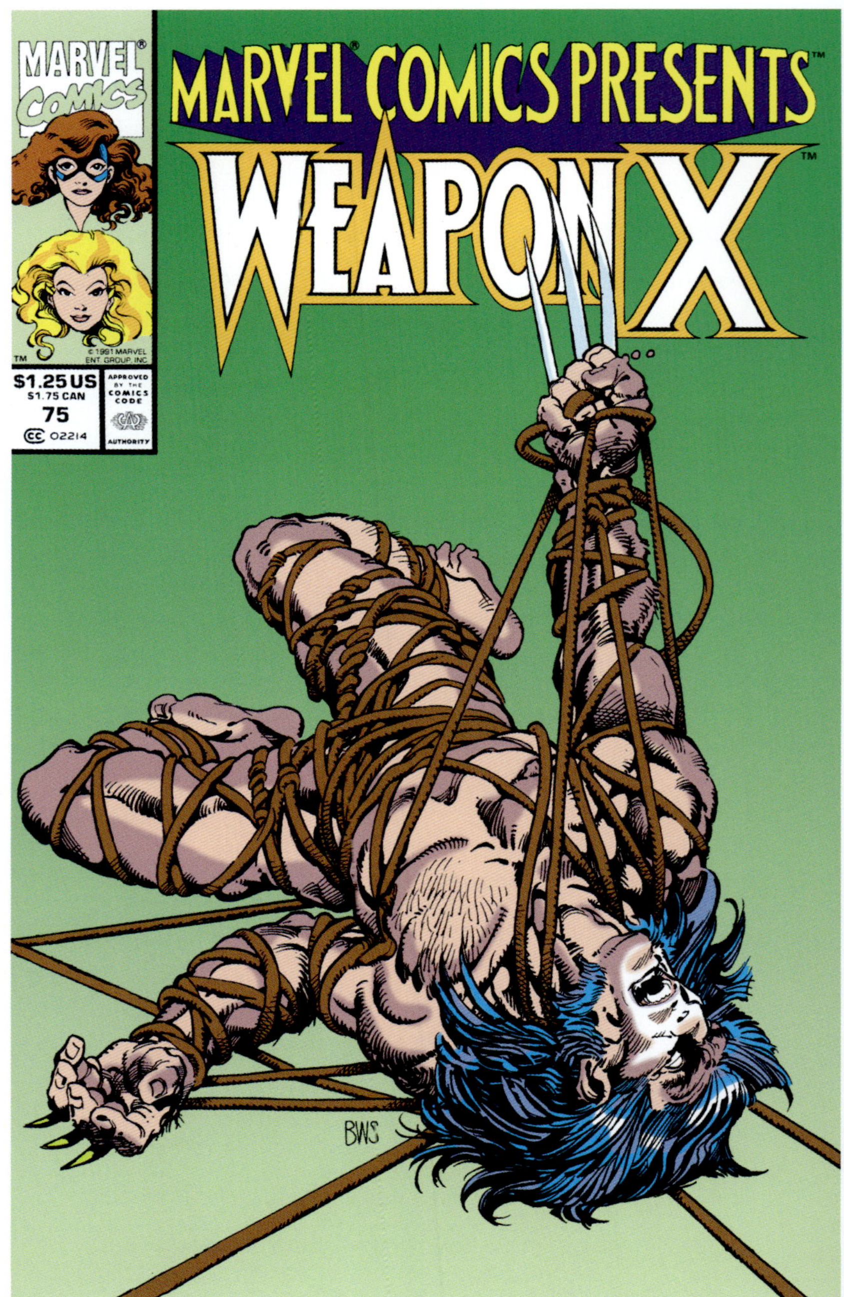
MARVEL COMICS
MARVEL COMICS PRESENTS
WEAPON X
© 1991 MARVEL ENT. GROUP, INC
$1.25 US
$1.75 CAN
75
CC 02214
APPROVED BY THE COMICS CODE AUTHORITY
BWS

This is the first use of the word "monster" in *Weapon X*. Descriptions of this story often reference *Frankenstein*. Barry Windsor-Smith spent three decades working on a graphic novel called *Monsters* (2022, Fantagraphics). While it is very different from *Weapon X*, both stories feature themes of monsters, men, trauma, and war.

Conversation between the Professor and Dr. Cornelius makes up the bulk of chapter three. The Professor demonstrates how cunning and manipulative he can be. Early in the chapter, he sympathizes with Cornelius to earn his trust. "You must have been terrified, Doctor!" At the end, he appeals to Cornelius' humanity to help Logan.

This 35-year-old scene feels very prescient with the cynical, skeptical way conspiracy theorists have come to view science and the medical and military industrial complex. As these scientific elites stand over an unconscious killer and his victim's dead body, they flaunt the law and morality and focus on their own professional goals with the experiment. They show zero compassion for the bloody bodies on the floor.

First, the Professor discounts the need for police involvement. Then he explains that the dead boys' family can be compensated. "Secured, let us say."

With that unfortunate business out of the way, he returns to the main subject of Experiment-X.

But before they make plans to "help" Logan, there is a

sequence where the Professor appeals to Cornelius to trust him. "Perhaps it is time to induct you further into my program —but I will require your explicit trust." While Cornelius is reeling from the traumatic situation he just survived, the Professor exploits his vulnerable state to bring him deeper into Experiment-X. This moment of manipulation is almost exactly the same as the plan that the Professor lays out for Logan. He is reprogramming Dr. Cornelius, "manipulation of the mindless…"

The Professor explains that Logan has lived like a violent individual his whole life "but now his demon is free – released by the intervention of Experiment-X. Thus…the double id is supplanted by the superego and all of Logan's primal instincts are focused and resolved. What you're looking at right now, doctor…is the most formidable tactical weapon ever conceived."

Logan wakes up briefly, but before he can attack, the Professor gasses him back into unconsciousness.

Cornelius recoils from this inhumane treatment of Logan and the Professor appeals to Dr. Cornelius to help save this "mindless, murdering animal." Both men use this phrase to refer to Logan. Regardless of their moral differences, they agree that Logan is an experiment—a lab animal: "Logan must be restructured now…trained. Then Programmed. You can do all of this. Manipulation of the mindless, Doctor Cornelius…it is your calling."

To continue the conspiratorial contextualization of this chapter, it is impossible not to see parallels between their conversation and the CIA's MK-Ultra mind control program from the 1950s–1970s. Although most of the MK-Ultra papers were allegedly destroyed, members of the CIA acknowledged the program to Congress under oath during the Church hearings of the 1970s. The program's goals included mind control, brainwashing, and the development of truth serum drugs amongst other allegations. This program was revealed in a series of *New York Times* articles in the 1970s.

When the Professor stands over Logan's unconscious body and describes him as "the most formidable tactical weapon ever conceived," it's hard not to imagine a mutant Manchurian candidate.

As the story continues, and the Experiment-X team keeps refining their weapon, the sense of Cold War, military-industrial-complex machinations grows ever stronger.

Weapon X…Chapter Four

> "Experiment X picks up the pace as Logan manifests his claws…"

For the second chapter in a row, "monster" appears on the opening page: "Create a monster."

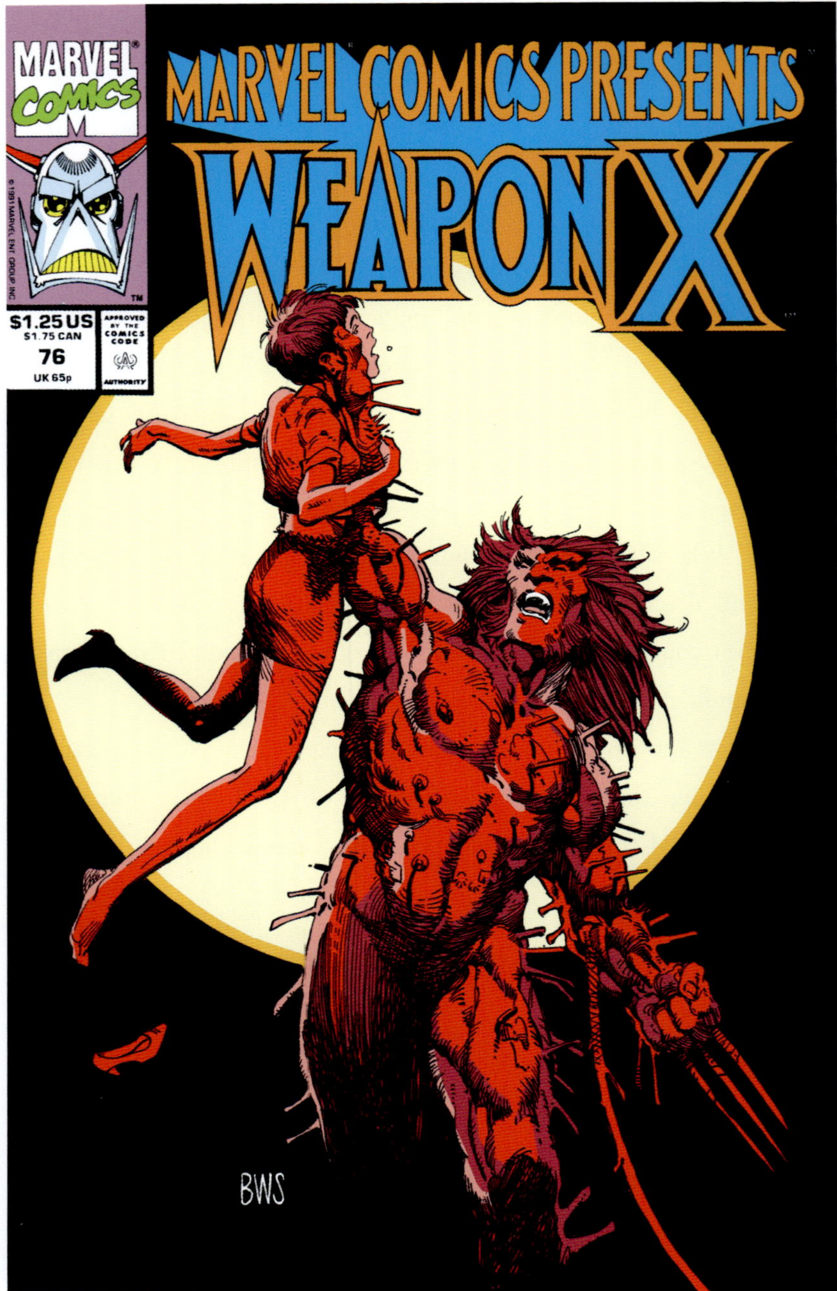
MARVEL
COMICS
© 1991 MARVEL ENT. GROUP INC.
$1.25 US
$1.75 CAN
76
UK 65p
APPROVED BY THE COMICS CODE AUTHORITY
MARVEL COMICS PRESENTS
WEAPON X
BWS

The cover features Logan attacking Hines. The figures are bathed in red ink. Logan's long hair makes him look like a nightmarish version of a Thundercat. The 1980s slasher movie motif is strong here.

The splash panel reveals more cables and tubes. Logan lays in a technological sarcophagus surrounded by wires, computer monitors, and the legacy of Kirby tech. In *Comics Scene* 18, Barry Windsor-Smith described this story as "about as bloody scientific as the Hulk being zapped by gamma rays!" This splash panel feels like the visual equivalent of that statement. These wires and medical tech are textures and patterns. Their meaning is not narrative or scientific, it is graphomania. And it is glorious!

Hines and Cornelius face the readers. Logan's body separates them from the Professor. His back is to the reader. This arrangement visually continues the rift between the Professor and Dr. Cornelius that began in chapter three and it establishes Hines on Cornelius' side. This dynamic continues throughout the story.

There is a lot of rumor and back story behind *Weapon X*. The story was first mentioned in *Comic Shop News* 56, which had a July 27, 1988 cover date but was not published until 1991. In interviews, Windsor-Smith stated that the story chapters were done out of sequence. He was also in a car accident that interrupted work on the story for six months. The result of

these events is that many of the chapters look and feel different from each other. Windsor-Smith has stated that he drew the story in different styles. This chapter features panels that are separated by a single line, rather than a line, gutter space, and another line. This may not be a major narrative choice, but it does create dissonance between panels that affects the reading experience. It is unclear how much time passes between many of the chapters. Has the POV of the narrative changed? These minor differences add to the overall unsettling atmosphere of *Weapon X*. With this chapter, the narrative begins to feel more subjective. It becomes harder to determine what is "real" in this story.

This kind of fractured narrative approach adds to the atmosphere and tone of *Weapon X*. It recalls storytelling that is common in the conspiracy theory genre. It feels incomplete—a trope of the genre is the reader's limited perspective. Like a whistleblower giving away some important piece of information, but where the whole story remains unclear. We can't see the big picture. We do not know all who are involved or the size and scope of the project. Windsor-Smith uses a similar style in *Weapon X*. The brevity of the story may add to this overall effect. Reading *Weapon X* does not feel like an exhaustive, answer-filled text about how Wolverine got his metal skeleton. It feels like the tip of the iceberg. That tone of paranoia and questions about the nature of reality in the story is uncanny at times and uncommon for Marvel comics.

Unlike the previous installments, this chapter is linear and takes place in one location, the lab. Hines and Cornelius prep Logan for the Professor's control. As the Professor explains, "what's the point of this weapon if we can't control him?"

A large screen is connected to Logan. It will function in

direct relation to the Professor's spoken word so that everyone can see what Logan is thinking as he receives input.

But before Experiment-X can try to control Logan, feedback overloads the computers. Then monstrous images appear on the screen and words. Logan speaks in single words on screen and then in person as he stirs from the operating table.

"Uhn…"

"Aaarr!"

"I…hurting…"

"PAIN!"

The images on the screen make an incredible set piece as the Professor, Cornelius, and Hines find themselves between big-screen, nightmarish images from inside of Logan's head and Logan himself starting to violently rampage.

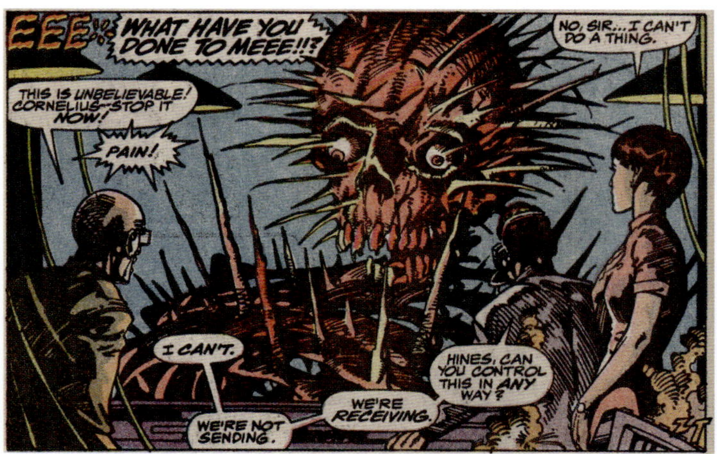

"WHAT HAVE YOU DONE TO MEEE!!?"

One of the most disturbing and imaginative drawings of the entire story is an inhuman creature that looks like it is made up of a couple of beings merged together. The panel features screaming onomatopoeia at the top and bottom and word balloons expressing Logan's pain and hurting.

As Logan wakes up, he grabs Hines' throat, probably because she is the closest person. Cornelius calls for security and the Professor tries to command Logan.

Logan resists the Professor's attempts at mind control although Logan does not seem to be in total control of himself. He growls rather than speaks as he throws Hines aside and grabs the Professor's throat.

Before he can kill the Professor, security shoots Logan with tranquilizers. An unconscious Logan reflexively extends his claws.

This chapter features Hines more than any previous chapter. She is responsible for the programming that is supposed to allow control over Logan. She is also the first of the three main characters that Logan lays his hands on.

The Professor's reaction to Logan's outburst is to order Logan killed.

This is classic cowardly villain behavior. The Professor had no sympathy for the young tech that Logan killed in chapter two. He offered a little sympathy to Dr. Cornelius after Logan lunged at him in chapter three, but that seemed to be in part to manipulate the doctor. But once Logan threatens the Professor, his entire tone changes. It's a great moment as it reverses the power dynamics that have dominated the story so far. "The

most formidable tactical weapon ever conceived" may be more dangerous and harder to control than the mad scientists thought. It also changes the dynamics between the Professor and Dr. Cornelius. Cornelius takes control briefly. He orders the guards to get medical staff and tells the Professor to calm down because he's in shock.

This chapter ends with Hines calling everyone's attention to a clear image on the big monitor screen. The image is a close-up of the Professor's dead, bloody face with claw marks through his eyes. Is this an image of things to come or merely the fantasy of a drugged-up lab animal?

Weapon X…Chapter Five

> "Now that the Professor has worked up a complete psychological profile on Experiment X, he further inducts Cornelius into the project…"

Windsor-Smith's *Weapon X* covers are a striking body of work in and of themselves. This cover in particular stands out. It was featured as the back cover of the first edition of the Weapon X hardcover's dust jacket. The use of coloring to depict shadows on the snowy landscape is a beautiful detail. Rather than using ink lines, Windsor-Smith relies only on the color shapes. It calls to mind a technique that Chris Ware uses in his critical and

MARVEL COMICS
MARVEL COMICS PRESENTS
WEAPON X
© 1991 MARVEL ENT GROUP INC
$1.25 US
$1.75 CAN
77
UK 65p
APPROVED BY THE COMICS CODE AUTHORITY
BWS

commercial hit graphic novel *Jimmy Corrigan, the Smartest Kid on Earth* (2000, Pantheon), where he depicts snow-covered roofs and snowflakes without a black ink outline. This cover also offers a welcome break from the claustrophobic interiors featured in the first four chapters—not that the 15-degrees-below-zero Canadian winter landscape offers Logan any sort of reprieve.

Another chapter, another art style.

According to Windsor-Smith, "The first story I drew is chapter five now, but it's got a slightly different art style because I drew it slower and more fiddly" (*Amazing Heroes* 188, Feb 1991, p. 32).

Panel 1 is a close-up of a wolf's eyes with thick lines to indicate fur—more organic than the cross-hatching seen so far in the story. The splash panel shows Logan's bust. Wires and probes extend from him. His eyes are shut. He's covered in sheep's blood to provide a "quicker scent" for predators. "Ingenious," says the Professor. "Lovely."

Logan stands in the sub-zero Canadian wilderness at dawn. Snow covers the ground. Several cameras focus on him. He's naked except for a loincloth.

This is the first time that Logan is outside of the Experiment-X lab. The wilderness and dawn/early morning palette contrast against the harsh, metallic interiors of the previous chapter. The change in setting also illustrates the idea of Logan or Weapon X as an animal. Ultimately, comics are a visual medium, and the winter wilderness is a great environment for Windsor-Smith to show off his drawing and color skills. Despite the violence of this chapter, the beauty of the artwork shines brightly.

The Experiment-X team watches the proceedings from the lab's monitors over morning coffee and danishes.

"Well, doctor, show me what Weapon X can do…"

The command is given to release the gates. A pack of hungry wolves run towards Weapon X. They have not eaten in six days.

Weapon X stands still. The wolves attack him. The Professor fears the wolves will rip him apart but then his claws extend and he begins screaming. The savagery is extreme. Hines asks if they can stop it and save the animals?

It's a "total massacre!"

"Bone…bonded to the hardest metal in the world—inside the body of a berserker!"

"Gentlemen, we have succeeded!"

"The perfect killing machine."

Weapon X, now covered in sheep's blood, his own blood, and the wolves' blood, stands above the carnage, claws out—roaring!

The Professor is ecstatic, his mood tempered only by his disappointment that they don't have any more wolves to

sacrifice. He is elated by what he has just witnessed. Hines turns away from the screen, repulsed. It is a dramatic contrast from the previous chapter when the Professor turned away and Hines stared at the screen depicting Logan's murder fantasy.

The Professor tells Cornelius to turn him off and Weapon X collapses on top of the pile of carcasses.

When Cornelius tells the wranglers to bring him in, the Professor tells him to leave him out for the night—despite the 15 degrees below zero temperature.

"Leave Logan out for the night…I like the idea of him resting in his own gore."

The chapter ends with the wranglers collaring Logan the following morning. They use long-handled poles that wrap around his neck to lead him back to the laboratory. The Professor tells them to bring him in.

"We have many more trials for Weapon X."

This is the first chapter that refers to Logan as Weapon X.

It is an escalation of his dehumanization by the Professor and his team. Previously, the Professor described him as a mutant, not human. He began as an experiment. And now that the Professor is learning more about this experiment and what Logan is capable of, he's referring to him as "the perfect killing machine" and as Weapon X.

The story is not just graphic violence. It is psychologically brutal in the dehumanizing treatment of the Logan character. The elation of the Professor in contrast with the suffering of Logan is pure depravity. The goal is not just to physically transform Logan but also to mentally and emotionally erase Logan in order to create Weapon X. It is a far cry from Steve Rogers volunteering for the super soldier experiments that led to Captain America—a tale of two super hero origins that illustrate the pre-World War II and post-Vietnam American psyche.

Weapon X…Chapter Six

> "Logan has survived Experiment X's first field test, teaching the Professor more than he wanted to know…"

On first impression, this chapter is another shift in art style. Is this the mature part of *Weapon X* stylistically or was this an early chapter?

MARVEL COMICS
MARVEL COMICS PRESENTS
WEAPON X
$1.25 US
$1.75 CAN
78
UK 65p
APPROVED BY THE COMICS CODE AUTHORITY
BWS

Red circles form a pattern behind the noir-shadowed faces of Cornelius and the Professor. The circles break from the Pete Mondrian squares and rectangles, adding another shape to psychedelic patterns and colors for backgrounds.

The tone of this chapter also feels a little different than the previous chapters. There are a few panels of physical comedy. They stand out against the overall horrors of the majority of *Weapon X*.

The experimenters continue to update Weapon X.

The Professor wants to be able to control him remotely up to a ten-mile radius. He wants a physical interface, like an arcade game (my words, not his), and when Weapon X is not turned on, he wants him unconscious and no threat to the Professor.

To accomplish this, technicians operate on Logan. They keep him in a semiconscious state for pseudo-scientific reasons. Dr. Cornelius explains how painful this must be for Logan.

On page 2, Weapon X appears to be crucified upside down on the operating table. Yes. This book has the Comics Code Approval stamp on the cover. I just double checked. What a shameful, fraudulent organization. That *A* is a scarlet letter on the history of comics.

When the Professor first tries to control Weapon X, the effects are awkward. He walks like a zombie and overreacts to the Professor's inputs. The staff laugh, humiliating the Professor. Afterwards, he shares a moment with Cornelius and we learn

SO, THE SUTURES ARE ALL HEALED, ARE THEY?
NOT QUITE, PROFESSOR--
--BUT ENOUGH FOR THIS PURPOSE.
WE COULD WAIT A FEW MINUTES IF YOU'D PREFER.
NO, NO. LET'S GET ON WITH IT, CORNELIUS.
OKAY, THE CABLES AREN'T A PROBLEM, THEY CAN BE REDUCED LATER. THE POWER SOURCE AND RECEIVERS ARE TEMPORARY. WE'LL TRY TO COMPACT THE BOXES--BUT I CAN'T GUARANTEE THAT.
FOR ANYTHING OVER, SAY-- HUNDRED AND FIFTY YARDS, WE'LL NEED THE HELMET DEVICE TO PULL IN THE SIGNAL.
UHM...
...OTHER THAN THAT, WE'RE IN BUSINESS.
AND WHAT OF THE RANGE, CORNELIUS?
A LITTLE OVER NINE MILES, SIR.
HMPH!
AND THE CONTROL CONSOLE, HERE? IT ISN'T FROM MY DESIGN.
YOU WANTED THE EXTRA POWER, SIR, WE HAD TO MODIFY--
STAFF, SHOW THE PROFESSOR THE LAYOUT OF YOUR TOP BOARD.
SURE, OKAY.

that the Professor is shaken from Weapon X attacking him. Cornelius tells him to spit in his eye.

Instead, we get a full-page sequence of the Professor dumping hot coffee on Weapon X's unconscious face. The wranglers can clean it up.

The coffee splashes and pools on his face and the reddish brown color looks like blood as we close the chapter with the Professor staring down at the pitiful-looking Logan, naked, wires and batteries hanging off of him, and coffee all over his face.

Oddly, two of the panels are repeated three times on this page. One of the panels is the Professor's head, looking down. The other is a close-up of Weapon X's eye. Drawn on the eye are three different states of a coffee drop as it hits the eye, then starts to roll, and finally runs down his face. Is this a reference to Bernie Krigstein's EC Comics masterpiece, "Master Race"? The Professor looks eerily similar to the ex-Nazi guard in that story; even the linework on the Professor's suit is similar. The other similarity is that Windsor-Smith uses time in an unusual way in Weapon X. Krigstein depicts time passing within a panel using an unusual drawing technique to show a subway train's motion: In several panels, Krigstein draws the motion of the subway train by repeatedly drawing the subway train several times in the same panel.

Bernie Krigstein is one of the most celebrated artists to

CONTINUES NEXT ISSUE...

work in comics. His best-known stories were published by EC Comics, a Golden Age publisher that was effectively canceled by the Comics Code Authority in the mid-1950s. EC Comics paid the best page rates in the industry and as a result, their regular artists were some of the highest regarded illustrators in the industry. After they stopped publishing comic books, their stories were reprinted by other publishers in every decade from the 1970s. Did Windsor-Smith see Krigstein's "Master Race" comic? In 1974, a special issue of *Squa Tront,* an EC fanzine, was published that featured the work of Bernie Krigstein. It included a lengthy essay on "Master Race" that was co-authored by Art Spiegelman (who would go on to win a Pulitzer Prize for his graphic novel *Maus*). In the 1970s, Windsor-Smith was self-publishing under the name Gorblimey Press. He may have used the same distributors as *Squa Tront*. Leaders in a field often know each other. At that time, self-publishing was not common. And like Windsor-Smith, Krigstein left comics to pursue painting. "Master Race" was also reprinted in *The Smithsonian Book of Comic Books* in 1981, which was widely available. And it is known to be an influence on a number of influential cartoonists including Spiegelman, Frank Miller, and Dan Clowes. It is likely that Windsor-Smith was familiar with Krigstein's "Master Race" story. There are some striking visual parallels but they could be coincidental.

Weapon X…Chapter Seven

"The Professor has fine-tuned his control over Experiment X…or has he?"

Another iconic cover, this art was featured on 2021's *Wolverine: Weapon X Gallery Edition* and 2023's *Wolverine: Weapon X Deluxe Edition*. The use of red blood was rare for a book with the Comics Code Authority stamp. But by 1991, the organization was practically irrelevant. They continued collecting payment from the last couple of publishers that still used them, but their power had waned to the point of complete meaninglessness by this time. The direct market system surpassed news-stand distribution in 1986. Marvel and DC had published books without the Code's stamp of approval. According to Terry Kavanagh, the editor of *Weapon X*, the only complaint he heard from the Comics Code Authority was to avoid showing too much of Wolverine's naked thigh. As for this cover, it has become one of the most widely used and celebrated pieces of Windsor-Smith's *Weapon X* art.

In this chapter, Weapon X dons his helmet and decapitates a grizzly bear in another successful field test—an "utterly impeccable killing!" The weapon is being honed. It only takes three pages to dispatch the bear.

While the team is pleased with Weapon X's performance and

MARVEL COMICS
MARVEL COMICS PRESENTS
WEAPON X
$1.25 US
$1.75 CAN
79
UK 65p
APPROVED BY THE COMICS CODE AUTHORITY
BWS

their control over him, the Professor is eager to test his weapon on the most dangerous game of all—man! Dr. Cornelius voices his objections to the Professor.

After the Professor leaves, Dr. Cornelius confides in Hines that he is uncomfortable with this latest development. He's not capable of murder. Hines appears willing to back Cornelius, but before they can make a plan, Weapon X kills a guard and cuts his way out of Laboratory 2.

The alarms sound! Cornelius blames the Professor. But the

HEARTRATE UP...
ADRENAL RISE WITH CARPAL FLUX...
LEFT CLAW EXTRUSION.
CAMERA TEN, PLEASE.
SWITCHING.
THIS IS IT!
KEEP IT RUNNING, HINES--
WE WON'T GET A SECOND CHANCE!
UH!
MISTER LOGAN SET!--
UH--
I MEAN...
WEAPONEX SET TWELVE
STIMULUS RESPONSE: QUARRY ONE...
DURATION FROM ZERO: FOUR

Professor denies that he is in control of this. If he isn't doing it, then who is in control of Weapon X? And how can anyone stop a "perfect killing machine"? This is slasher movies 101. They made the "perfect killing machine" and now it's out of control and coming their way!

There is a lot of iconic imagery in this chapter, starting with the cover. The grizzly bear fight mentioned above appeared in promotional outlets like *Comics Scene* 18.

Page one features the classic Weapon X design that would inspire action figure toys.

This chapter also plants the idea of Weapon X hunting man, and then ends with Weapon X killing his guards and heading for the control room! The Professor told Cornelius he wanted "action" and this chapter delivers it.

Coincidentally, the back cover of this issue is by Mike "Hellboy" Mignola and features a World War II story pitting Sgt. Fury and his Howling Commandos against Dracula! For good measure, there is a

2" swastika as well. Coincidence, no doubt. But it does fit the Nazi-esque references to human experimentation found in Weapon X as well as the previously mentioned EC Comics story, "Master Race."

Weapon X…Chapter Eight

> "Hines and Cornelius are having second thoughts about Experiment X – but it's too late…Logan is on the loose!"

This chapter is very action heavy and that action takes place in three locations. The Professor is in his office. Cornelius and Hines are in the lab. Weapon X and security move through the facility.

Weapon X, the perfect killing machine, is out of control. The Professor and Cornelius cannot stop him no matter what they try. Security shoots him with tranquilizers but they have no effect. They request permission to use artillery.

The Professor calls someone and accidentally leaves the intercom on so Hines and Cornelius hear part of the conversation. In this sequence, they share a similar perspective with readers. From this limited vantage point, it seems that the Professor's master may have some hand in Weapon X's killing spree.

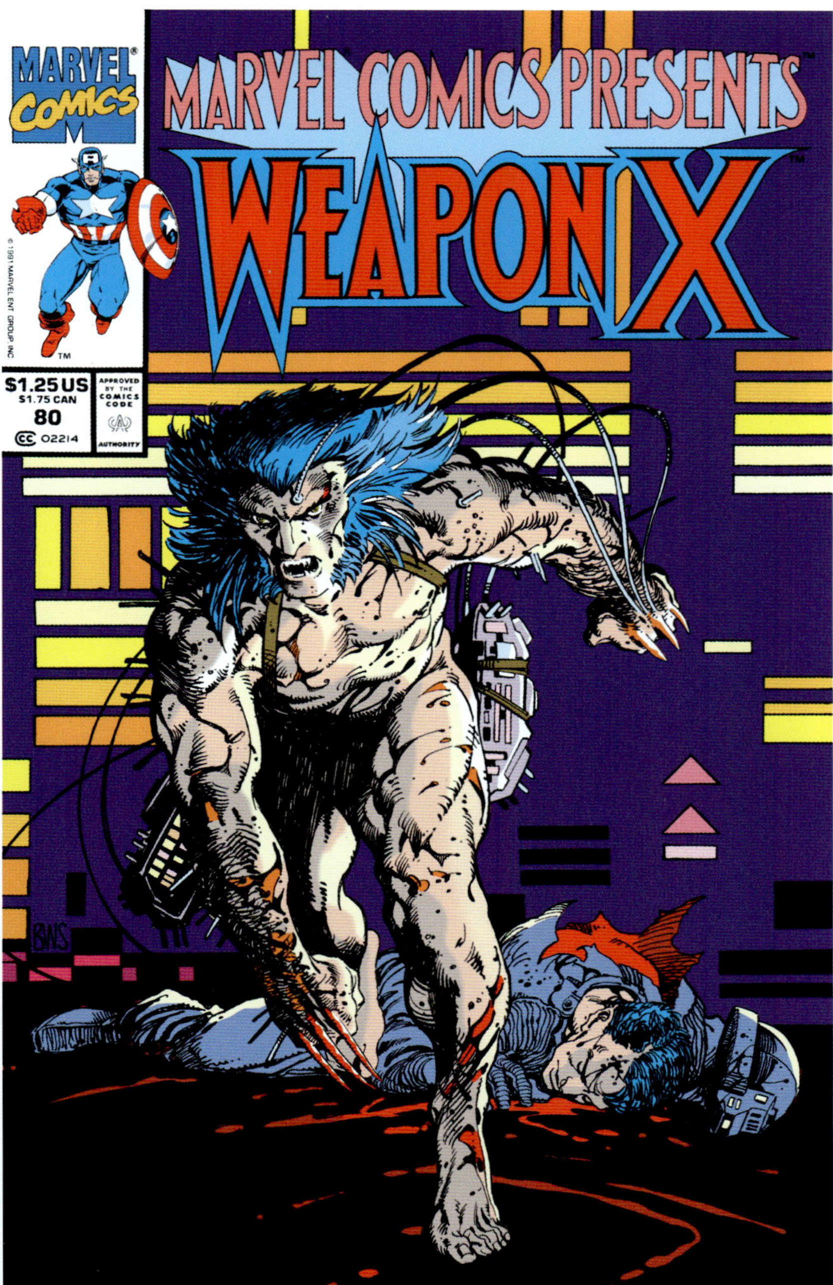
MARVEL COMICS
MARVEL COMICS PRESENTS
WEAPON X
© 1991 MARVEL ENT. GROUP, INC.
$1.25 US
$1.75 CAN
80
CC 02214
APPROVED BY THE COMICS CODE AUTHORITY
BWS

RUNNING AMOK, YOU MIGHT SAY.
PRECISELY. KILLING EVERYONE IN SIGHT ...HMMM...YES...
HINES--WHO'S HE TALKING TO?
YES, IT'S JUST THAT-- YOU SEE--LOGAN IS FULLY HARNESSED YET MY CONTROL PANELS ARE-- INACTIVE.
COMPUTER SHOWS... EXTERIOR UNIT, SIR!
BUT HE'S FORGOTTEN TO TURN OFF HIS INTERCOM.
DOC! FOR CRYIN' OUT LOUD! YA GOTTA OKAY THE WEAPONRY, I MEAN--SKAK--

I GOT MEN DOWN THERE POPPIN' PEA-SHOOTERS!
THEN GET 'EM OUTTA THERE, MAN--
FREEZE!
PDUM
PDM!

--BEFORE IT'S TOO LATE!
RRAH!

AAAAAAAAA
SECURITY! SK
SECURITY, ZONE THREE SKK
WE ARE LOSING OUR MARTIAL-GUARD SOMEWHAT PRECIPITATELY.
GET OUTTA THE TUNNELS!
AND, WHILST IT'S OF LITTLE CONCERN OVERALL--

The Professor asks whether he should leave or take refuge while Weapon X "clears the dead wood."

Simultaneously, the story follows Weapon X as he cuts through security. The body count is unclear. Weapon X killed a man in chapter two and one or two in the previous chapter. At one point, a security person says that five men are down. In *Weapon X*, the security team is treated like props. No one seems to care about the body count.

Weapon X enters service tunnels—echoes of the classic John Byrne Wolverine in tunnels under the Hellfire Club from *The Uncanny X-Men*.

Hines realizes that Weapon X is not moving randomly, his path is straight towards the Professor.

Cornelius authorizes artillery and he and Hines wait and listen as Weapon X and security converge on the Professor.

The chapter ends with the Professor on the ground, his hand cut off, and blood pouring out of his wrist onto his face—a

visual callback to end of chapter six when the Professor pours coffee on a prone Weapon X. The Professor screams, "KILL HIM! KILL!! DESTROY WEAPON X!"

Weapon X…Chapter Nine

> "Control of Project X has been taken out of the professor's hands – and Logan is on a rampage…"

Chapter nine's splash page features Weapon X in the middle of bodies. Blood covers the floor and sprays through the air. One body falls away from his right hand, claws extended and blood spraying out of the falling body. Another body is overhead. Weapon X's claws extend through this man's writhing torso. The color palette is mostly red. It's a massacre, a bloodbath. This image was used for one of the early collected editions of this story. It may be the image that most people think of when they think of *Weapon X*. The use of it on the trade paperback cemented its iconic status. It's a stunning image and I wonder why it was not used as a cover for *Marvel Comics Presents* 81. Maybe it was too graphic.

In this chapter, Weapon X has become the slasher. He destroys security personnel. There is a panel where Weapon X walks through the maimed and injured guards, killing the survivors one by one. The sound effects, hand-lettered by

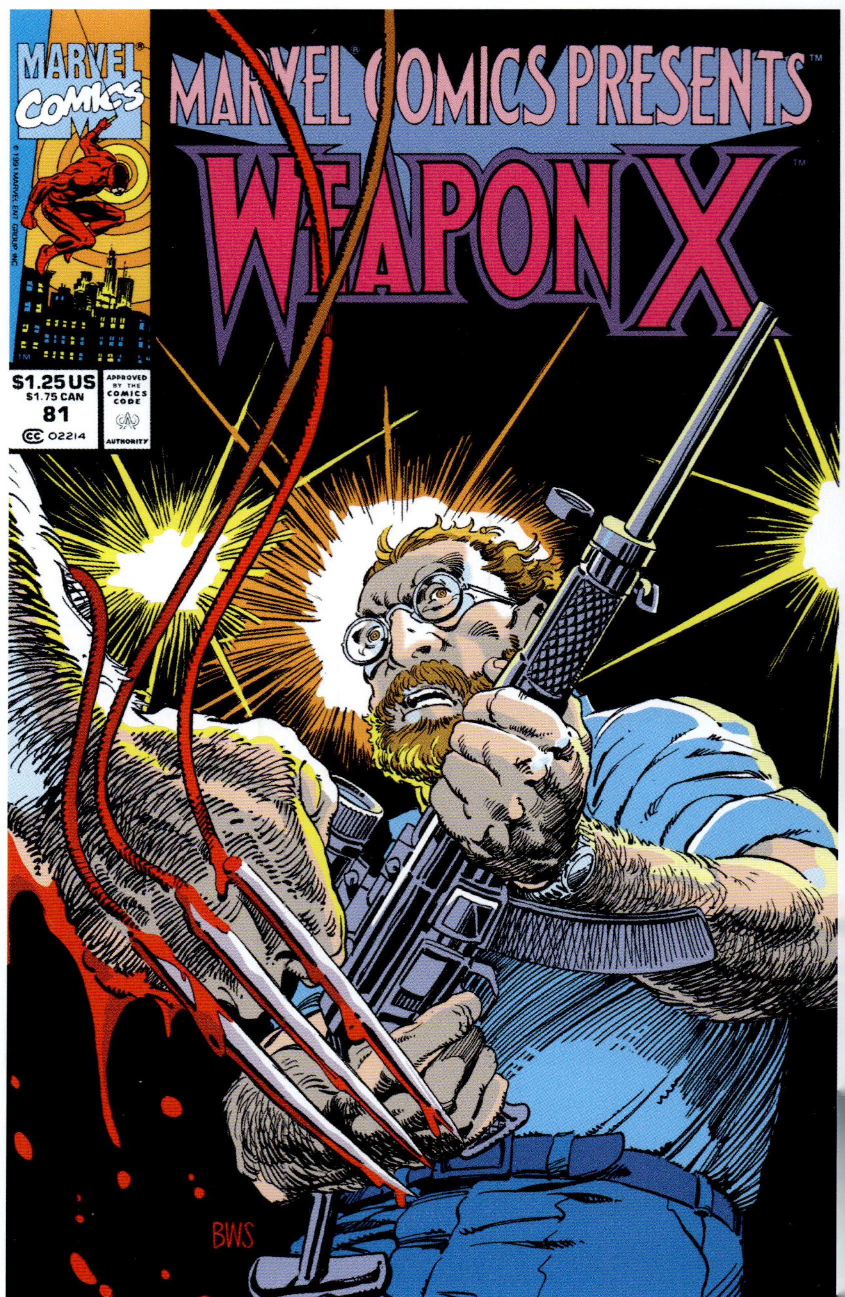

MARVEL COMICS
MARVEL COMICS PRESENTS
WEAPON X
© 1991 MARVEL ENT. GROUP, INC.
$1.25 US
$1.75 CAN
81
02214
APPROVED BY THE COMICS CODE AUTHORITY
BWS

DID YOU GET THE PROFESSOR OUT?!
SKK
DID YOU GET THE PROFESSOR OUT!? SK
ANSWER ME, SOMEBODY!!
WHAT'S GOIN' SK
PROF SECURED!
HE'S OKAY!
TARGET'S ALL OVER THE PLACE--!
NO CLEAR SHOTS--
LOSING MEN--
GET BACK FROM HIM SK
TOO LATE!
DOZEN BODY SHOTS-- NO EFFECT!
THIS IS A MASSACRE!
SKK FALL BACK SK FALL BACK!!
SK
SK

Windsor-Smith, are "SHIV," "SHLUK," and "SHLK," the sound of claws stabbing humans to death. A helpless soldier in the corner of the panel narrates his own death as Weapon X comes for him.

Dr. Cornelius and Hines bandage the Professor's arm stump. The three of them seek refuge in the adamantium core, where there is risk of meltdown, radiation, and blowing up. It is behind a door with a radiation logo warning. In comics, it is hard to see this logo and not think of *Watchmen*. The Professor acknowledges that someone else is in control of Weapon X and they are all "dead wood".

Weapon X tracks them down quickly and cuts his way through a wall to breach their short-lived, false hope of security.

The final page is another splash page—Weapon X, bloody, naked, and screaming like a hairy, wild animal towers over the

CONTINUES NEXT ISSUE...

Professor! This may be the most disturbing image of a super hero that Marvel has ever published—pure nightmare.

Windsor-Smith proved adept at working on eight-page installments and took advantage of this to tell a variety of stories. Some build on previous chapters' cliffhangers, some are more concerned with the visceral side of the characters' experience, and some feel like standalone short stories. What they have in common is that each chapter delivers new story information and a satisfying reading experience.

This chapter in particular stands out as an example of how much Windsor-Smith could do in eight pages. Despite two stunning full-page splashes, chapter nine covers a lot of ground. The main characters escape one bloody massacre and find a new location for a last stand. It began with the main characters spread through three locations and concludes with all of them together! This is also how the story opened.

This chapter makes clear that the Professor has been working with an unidentified superior. It's also clear that the mysterious superior does not value the Professor's life, just as the Professor doesn't value the lives of those serving under him.

Chapter nine showcases Weapon X's capability. Even with real bullets, the security team barely slows Weapon X down. The Professor, Cornelius, and Hines know that Weapon X is coming for them. It's a great example of show, don't tell. Up to this point, the story has talked about Weapon X's potential. In chapter seven, the Professor expressed his desire to see Weapon X tested against man. Be careful what you wish for. This chapter shows everybody what a perfect killing machine looks like in action.

It is a terrifying portrait of what super heroes had become by the early 1990s.

Weapon X…Chapter Ten

> "As Logan stalks the Professor, the terrified Professor tries in vain to contact his mysterious project leader…"

Weapon X stands motionless in front of the Professor, Cornelius, and Hines. The Professor commands Cornelius to shoot Weapon X. He does. Before he can shoot away the power packs, Weapon X kills him. Claws through the chest.

Cornelius' death allows the Professor and Hines to reach the adamantium reactor core. If they can lure Weapon X into the core, they can incinerate him!

The Professor decides that Hines is the best bait and pushes her into the reactor's core—a pit-like structure. He's careful not to drop her on her head, since he needs her to scream and yell. She can't do that if she breaks her neck falling into the core. He may be a cowardly villain but he is not stupid.

MARVEL COMICS
MARVEL COMICS PRESENTS
WEAPON X
$1.25 US
$1.75 CAN
82
02214
APPROVED BY THE COMICS CODE AUTHORITY
BWS

Hines screams, Weapon X appears, and the Professor begins the process of opening the fission-gate and purging.

The Professor stays true to his nature as he sacrifices Cornelius and Hines for his own survival.

Weapon X…Chapter Eleven

> "Using Ms. Hines as bait, the Professor has set a trap for the rogue Logan in the Fission Exhaust Pit…"

As Weapon X approaches, Hines begs him to "kill [her] quickly!"

Weapon X speaks. The lettering is different from the lettering for other characters' dialogue. It's a combination of upper and lower case, as well as ellipses between words. Is Logan breaking free of other people's control? Before we can find out, the Professor opens the fission-gate to purge Weapon X and Hines from this world.

Fire rains down on Weapon X.

But the full purge is interrupted. The Professor's mysterious leader overrides the order and stops the purge process.

As the Professor argues with his mysterious leader, a fiery figure climbs out of the exhaust pit. Weapon X refuses to die and enters the Professor's control room. His hair has been burned from his body. Flames still burn on his skin.

MARVEL COMICS
MARVEL COMICS PRESENTS
WEAPON X
© 1991 MARVEL ENT. GROUP, INC.
$1.25 US
$1.75 CAN
83
02214
APPROVED BY THE COMICS CODE AUTHORITY

DeAd?
WAlk-ing
Dea d Man?
aM I?

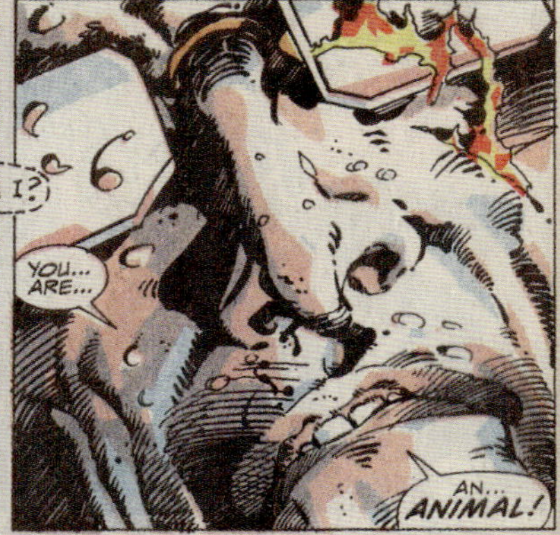

YOU...
ARE...
AN...
ANIMAL!

I AM--
LOGAN!
AAARHH!
uhhnn
uh-uH!
LOGAN!
I AM
A MAN!

AND
YOU--
UHK
--ARE THE
ANIMAL!
K-CHASH

WELL...IT DON'T.
AAEEEE!
UGHUH
NUH
UHN
NUH!

SNIKKUDK!

SNIKZHUKT!

SNIKT
ZHDUK!

NOW...WE'RE ...SQUARE.
GOT THAT... CHUMP?
SPECIAL TRIPLE-SIZED CONCLUSION NEXT ISSUE...

He screams that he is Logan and he is a man, not an animal!

Logan cuts off the Professor's left hand. Both wrists are now severed.

Finally, he puts three claws through the Professor's face and out the back of his skull. Blood pours out of his head.

Weapon X…Chapter Twelve

> "Logan has destroyed most of Project X, including the Professor…or has he?"

The final chapter of *Weapon X* is 24 pages long. Triple-sized! It occupies the first 75 percent of *Marvel Comics Presents* 84. It features a wraparound cover of a close-up illustration by Windsor-Smith of Logan's face. Logan's eyes are closed. His face is covered in blood. Logan holds his hands up. They are also covered in blood. Bloody claws protrude from his hands. The color is a limited palette of magenta and yellow that looks mostly orange.

The chapter begins where chapter eleven stopped. Weapon X throws the Professor's dead body into the fire of the exhaust pipe.

Cut to black.

Weapon X wakes up on the floor of the control room where he killed the Professor. There appears to be a random playback

of audio that features dialogue from previous chapters. Before he leaves the control room, he sees the Professor's severed hand—the hand that Weapon X cut off in chapter eleven.

When Weapon X wakes up, he is completely naked. There are no wires, tubes, power packs, or a helmet. He also has long hair and hairy forearms. In chapter eleven, he was hairless from being burned in the exhaust pipe of the adamantium reactor core. Some period of time must have passed.

As he regains his senses, Weapon X tries to figure out where he is: "industrial…maybe military –" This explicit reference to the military-industrial complex leaves little room for debate about the conspiratorial subtext of *Weapon X*.

Weapon X or Logan compares the facility to a maze and

a tomb and decides it's too sharp for the military. "These computers are Buck Rogers." That is a perfect description of the backgrounds. It feels like 1970s movie and TV sci-fi with its sparse backgrounds of light patterns. But what version of Buck Rogers is Weapon X referring to? The comic strips that ran from 1929–1967? The serials of 1950? The TV series of 1979? None of these timelines fit Weapon X's nebulous setting, which according to Google and cbr.com is 1964. In *Amazing Heroes* 188 (Feb 1991, p. 31), Windsor-Smith says Weapon X "starts out sometime in the early '60s. I couldn't be bothered trying to figure out when it would be. It's in the early '60s."

Weapon X passes Cornelius' body—the doctor that he killed in chapter eleven. His memory returns. He says that they found him out—that he's a mutant. They tortured him, tore up his mind, got into his body. He's gotta get away!

As he runs from Experiment-X, he appears to be running into a dreamscape. The dialogue literally says this, "Runnin' in a DREAM!" As the pages progress, this dreamscape becomes more and more nightmarish as spikes extend from Weapon X and threaten to crush him under their weight.

The panels fade to black as Weapon X grows smaller and smaller until he is gone.

When the light returns, so have the voices of the Professor, Dr. Cornelius, and Hines. Weapon X emerges from a hole in a chain link fence and comes face to face with a Siberian tiger.

I'M RUNNIN'!
RUNNIN' IN A DREAM!
I GOT STICKS FOR LEGS AN' MY FEET ARE PUTTY!
AN' SOMETHING'S BEHIND ME!
MOVIN' WITH ME!

LIKE A LIVIN' SHADOW--
--IT'S AT MY HEELS...
...AND IF I SLOW DOWN IT'LL GET ME--
--I'LL SUFFOCATE IN IT--
--IN ITS DARKNESS!

AN' I WON'T BE ABLE TO SCREAM...
...OR YELL...
...OR FIGHT IT OFF.
'COS IT'LL BE INSIDE ME!

UNDER MY SKIN--
--IN MY GUTS--
--INSIDE MY BONES!
I'M RUNNIN' LIKE A TRUCK--A BARRELIN' TRUCK--AN' I'M UPHILL WITH A FULL LOAD. AN' THE THING'S BEHIND ME AN' IT'S GAININ' ALL THE TIME. I'M PUMPIN' AN' PUMPIN' BUT LOSIN' GROUND!

IT'S GRABBIN' AT ME--

SNATCHIN' AT MY VEINS LIKE ROPES, PULLIN' ME BACK, TENDONS LIKE WIRES--LIKE A PUPPET.

FINGERS PULLIN' THROUGH MY RIBS.

MUSCLES STRETCHIN'-- BONES BENDIN' BACK!

I'M RUNNIN'. I'M RUNNIN'.

IT'S TEARIN' AT ME-- DRAGGIN' ME BACK INTO ITS DARKNESS.

ENDLESS NIGHTMARE-- PITCHIN' WAVES RUNNIN' INTO THE NIGHT--LIQUID...

LIKE BLACK BLOOD.

AN' I CAN'T GET AWAY!

IT'S AT MY SHOULDER AN' IT'S CUTTIN' ME WITH SPIKES.

IT'S BREATHIN' INTO ME AN' I'M SUCKIN' ITS HOT BREATH.

STENCH OF DEATH IN MY MOUTH!

LUNGS HEAVIN'.

FINGERS CLAWIN'.

LEGS PUMPIN'.

AN' I CAN'T GET AWAY!

BUT I MUST--

RUN. RUN FOREVER--

FIGHT FOREVER!

NEVER GIVE IN!

THE BEAST!

OUT OF THE PITCH BLACK IT'S COMIN'--

CAN'T GO ON--
DON'T GIVE UP!
KNEES GIVIN IN--

GRISTLE SHOT--
DON'T GIVE UP!

EVERY THRUST--
BLOOD
AND
FIRE--

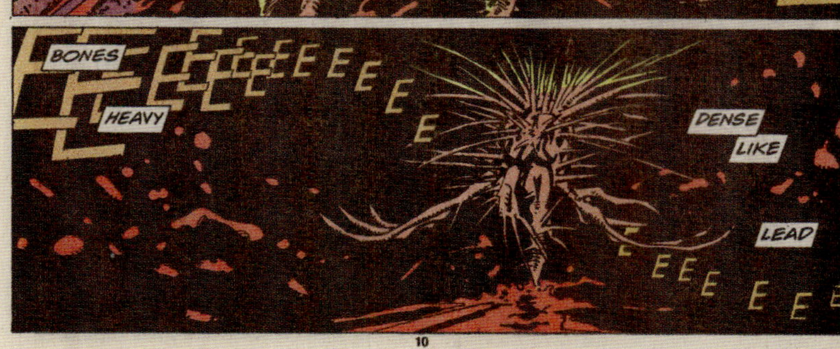
BONES
HEAVY
DENSE
LIKE
LEAD

The cool blues of the color palette in this scene defines the setting perfectly—a snow-covered forest landscape at night.

The tiger is not much of a match for Weapon X—the perfect killing machine. The Experiment-X team watches the battle unfold. In the aftermath, they discuss his behavior in the previous chapters. Apparently their deaths were a ruse that occurred in Weapon X's head, rather than real life. They order the wranglers to return Weapon X to his cage in D-Block.

When the narrative returns to Weapon X, dead wranglers lay in bloody snow while Weapon X walks back into the fenced area.

The Experiment-X team begins to panic when they cannot find Weapon X on camera and the wranglers don't respond. Claws breach their door. Weapon X cuts his way into the control room. Security is on the radio, trying to reach Hines, Cornelius, and the Professor but they do not respond as they face Weapon X.

The End

This last chapter adds mystery to the nature of *Weapon X*. What actually happened? If Experiment-X could make Weapon X believe he killed them once, is this really happening? And if killing the Experiment-X team was all in his head, what parts of this story are real and what aren't?

Pages 20–24 are titled "Interlude & Escape." Panel 1 is a

close-up of the Professor's broken, bloody glasses. Then we follow Weapon X through the snowy mountains. Colorful drawings appear in the sky, the aurora borealis or Northern Lights. As Weapon X's hair becomes snow and ice covered, captions reveal a conversation between Cornelius and Hines. They discuss Logan's participation in the project and his status as a mutant. Both express their regret of being a part of this project.

"Cheer up, Hinesy…be over soon."

Weapon X disappears into the snowy mountains.

The final panel is a shot of a bloody hand in the lab. Broken glass and fire surround it. Did Weapon X destroy the laboratory and program? Or is this another false memory? This open ending is for the reader to interpret.

5

Creator

Barry Windsor-Smith is credited as the writer, penciller, inker, colorist, and co-letterer of *Weapon X*. It is unusual for one person to perform all of these tasks in a Marvel comic book. The division of labor in comic book production can be traced to the early days of comic book publishing. From the 1930s–1950s, known as Comics Golden Age, comic book popularity exploded so publishers tried to make more comic books as fast as possible in order to capitalize on this new trend. Production houses sprung up to meet the demand, like the Eisner-Igor studios. Many of these production studios developed an assembly line system in order to create new comic book stories efficiently. The people working in this system specialized based on their skills, speed, and opportunity. This assembly line model continues to be used by many comic book publishers and creators. In a typical Marvel comic book in 1991, there would be a different person for each task: a writer, a penciller, an inker, a colorist, and a letterer. There are examples of individuals doing multiple tasks. Some people wrote and drew their own stories, like Jack Kirby, Will Eisner, Frank Miller, John Byrne, and Erik Larsen. Often pencillers would ink their own work like Todd McFarlane, Bill Sienkiewicz, Miller, Larsen, Byrne. Sometimes an inker would also color the work like Klaus Janson, Tom Palmer, and Kevin Nowlan, making them more of a finisher or illustrator. The vast majority of Marvel Comics were produced by teams of freelance creators.

Windsor-Smith was part of the second wave of the Marvel Universe. The Marvel Universe began in 1961 with the creation of the Fantastic Four by Jack Kirby and Stan Lee. Fantastic Four's success led to more and more super hero comics like Hulk, Avengers, Captain America, Thor, Iron Man, and X-Men. These were all created by Kirby and Lee. The other big creator for the initial Marvel Universe titles was Steve Ditko. Ditko and Stan Lee created Spider-Man and Dr. Strange. In the early 1960s, the comic book industry, including Marvel Comics, was facing difficult times. The creation of the Marvel Universe turned their company around. Growth followed that success and more artists were needed. Some of the artists were experienced cartoonists from the Golden Age while others were new. Barry Smith was new. He began working for Marvel in 1968.

At first, he was heavily influenced by Jack Kirby. This was not unusual as editor Stan Lee would often use Jack Kirby's work to show other artists what Lee wanted—specifically, dynamic action! As Smith gained experience, his style evolved and his art became more unique and less Kirbyesque.

In 1970, Marvel acquired the license for Robert E. Howard's *Conan the Barbarian*. Roy Thomas wrote the new comic and Barry Smith drew it. The first choice for artist was John Buscema. But Buscema's page rate was too high and Marvel was uncertain whether Conan would be successful, so they chose Smith because he cost less. The Conan comic book became a massive hit. Over the course of twenty-odd issues, Barry Smith's art developed rapidly into a fan-favorite style unlike anything else Marvel was publishing.

By the mid-1970s Smith had left comics. He was frustrated by the constraints of working in an art form that was aimed at children. Around this time, he added Windsor, his mother's surname, to Smith. Windsor-Smith studied painting, illustration, and printing. He started his own press, Gorblimey. And he joined Michael Kaluta, Bernie Wrightson, and Jeffrey Catherine Jones as part of a renowned group of comic book artists who began exploring and incorporating fine art and commercial illustration into their practices. They became known as the Studio. During this period, Barry Windsor-Smith evolved as an artist. His interest in Pre-Raphaelite art grew and he incorporated more line art and ornamental depictions of nature, architecture, and drapery into his figures and forms. This approach to line and color was very different from typical comic book art of the time (and still is). His anatomical illustration also continued to evolve.

Windsor-Smith returned to comic books in the 1980s. But he did not return to the monthly production schedule typical of most Marvel comic books at the time. Instead, he worked on mini-series, short stories, and single issues at a pace that allowed him to concentrate on the artwork. This approach was different and it made his comic books stand out on the newsstand or at the comic book shop. It reflected his growth as an artist. New Barry Windsor-Smith drawn comic books became special events because it did not happen every month. And when one appeared, it looked like Windsor-Smith poured his heart and soul into the artwork.

He illustrated and colored a *Machine Man* mini-series (with artist Herb Trimpe). He did fill-in issues for *Fantastic Four*, *Iron Man*, *Daredevil*, and *Excalibur*. A fill-in issue is an issue of an ongoing comic book series that features a different artist for an issue. Fill-in issues are often done to give the regular artist a break in their schedule. Windsor-Smith's style stood out against the style of other comic book artists, and fans responded. During this time, Windsor-Smith drew several issues of the popular *Uncanny X-Men* comic book, including issue 205, which featured Wolverine fighting cyborgs in a snow storm in

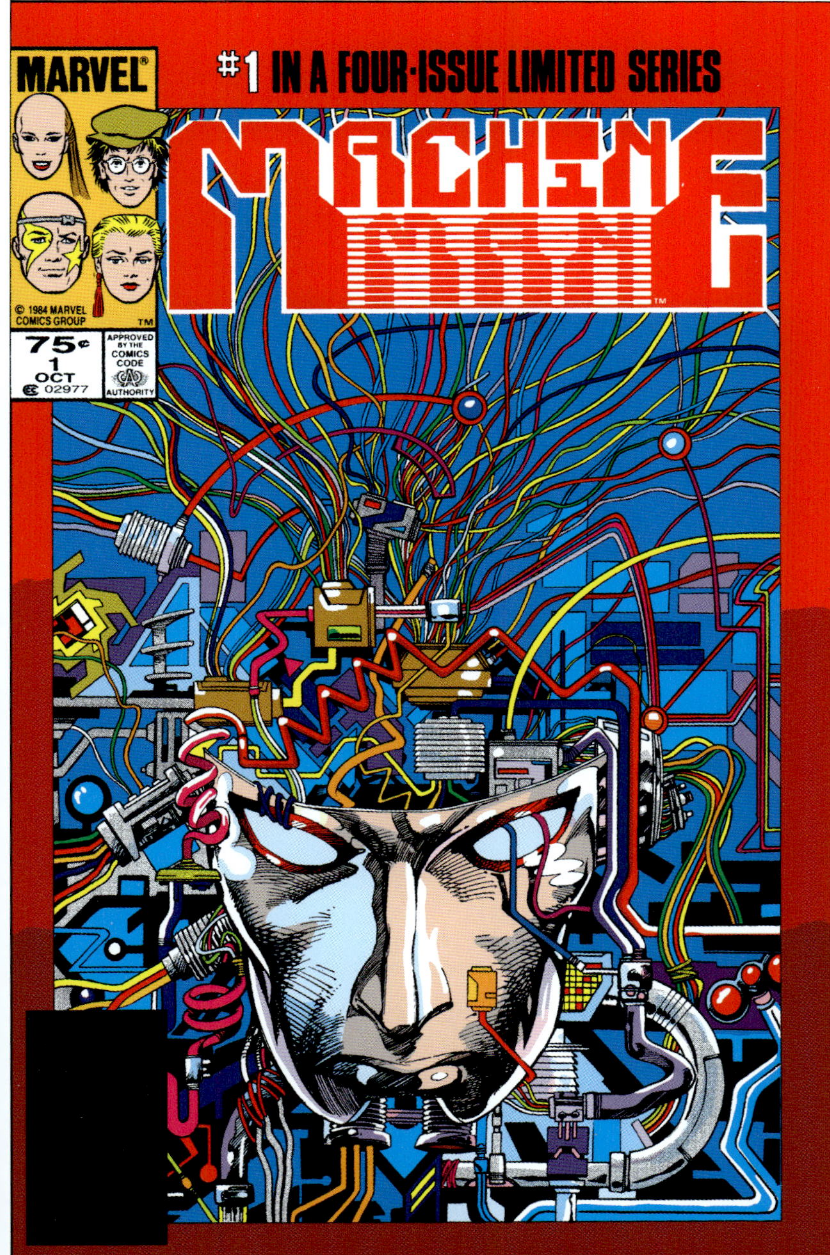

MARVEL®
#1 IN A FOUR-ISSUE LIMITED SERIES
MACHINE MAN
TM
© 1984 MARVEL COMICS GROUP
TM
75¢
1
OCT
02977
APPROVED BY THE COMICS CODE AUTHORITY

Central Park. The cover looks like a cover for *Weapon X* with wires and tubes, a prone Wolverine, and a striking magenta and purple color palette.

The assistant editor of X-Men at the time was Terry Kavanagh. In 1991, Terry Kavanagh was the editor of *Marvel Comics Presents*, the book where Weapon X was first published. As the editor of *Marvel Comics Presents*, Kavanagh approached Windsor-Smith about doing some work.

> Terry Kavanagh called me up one day and said, "I've got this script for *Marvel Comics Presents*"—I'd never heard of it—"would you like to draw it?" I forget what the story was, actually. And I said, "I don't know, send it off."
>
> It was an eight-page story, and while I didn't like the story, I liked the idea of doing little eight-page stories. I thought it was something rather concise and very testing of one's storytelling abilities: to do an eight-pager and make it sharp and hard rather than these meandering graphic novels.
>
> I was looking through *The Handbook to the Marvel Universe* and they mentioned he was once called "Weapon X." And I thought, "Well, there's a nifty title. What could I do with that?" And originally it was just going to be three or four, maybe five stories. Then, as the thing developed, it turned into a whole different thing.
>
> I didn't have a whole plot when I started. I just had a

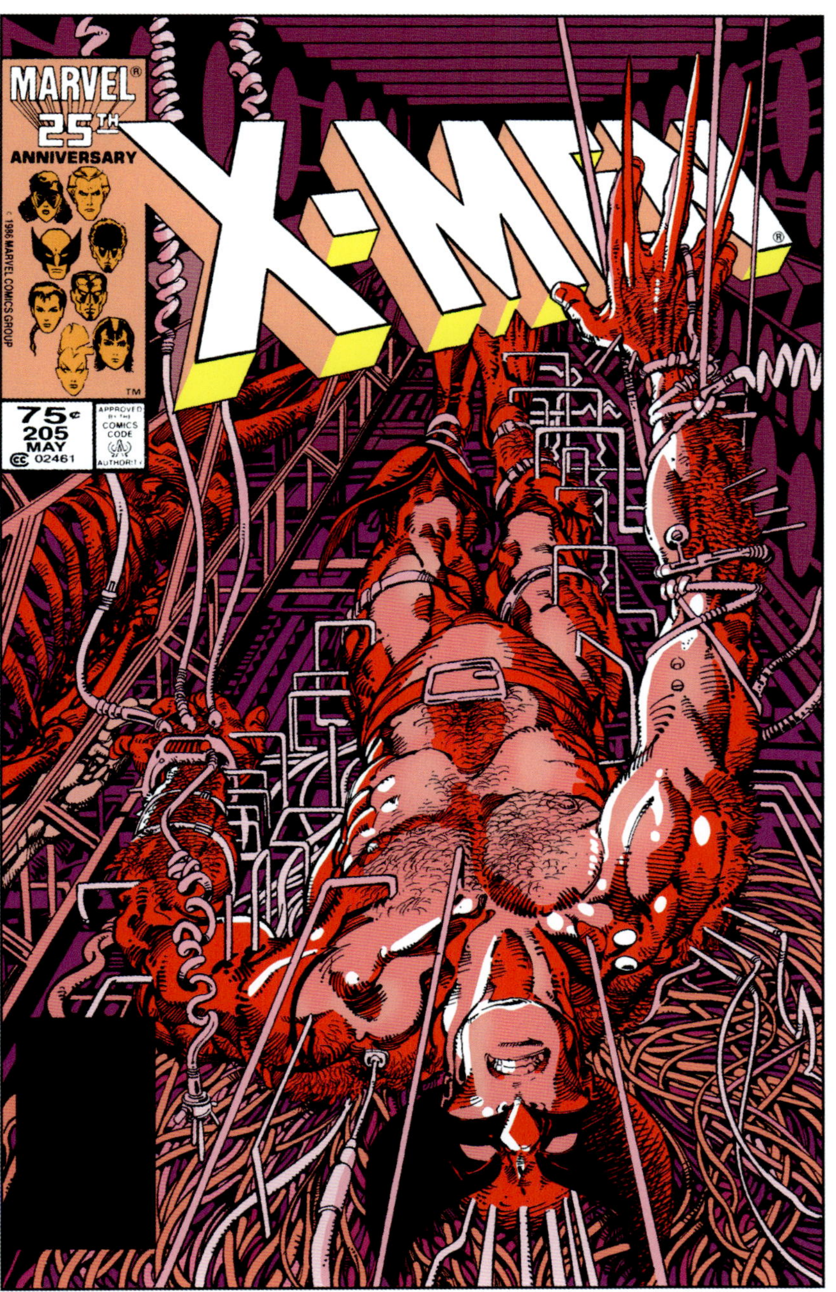

MARVEL®
25TH
ANNIVERSARY
© 1986 MARVEL COMICS GROUP
TM
X-M
75¢
205
MAY
CC 02461
APPROVED BY THE COMICS CODE AUTHORITY

> couple of story ideas and a general concept, and I didn't want to hang around and figure out a whole story. I kind of like not knowing what I'm going to do next. So once I talked to Terry and Tom DeFalco [then Marvel Editor-in-Chief] and committed myself to doing the series, I took down three stories to show them. They didn't even know I was doing it. I just called up Terry and said, "Listen, I've got this weird idea..." And he said, "Well, do you want to talk about it?" I said, "I'll show you this stuff...," and that's the way I work. (*Amazing Heroes* 188, Feb 1991, pp. 31, 32)

Barry Windsor-Smith stated in interviews during the promotion of *Weapon X* that he did not read comic books and he criticized the writing style of Marvel Comics.

> I quite deliberately chose to write it in a fashion that is distinctly non-Marvel. I simply refused to write Marvel-style, because [I find] it pitiable, to be honest with you. (*Wizard* Magazine 28, Dec 1993, p. 84)

By Marvel-style, I believe Windsor-Smith is referring to a show-and-tell approach where captions and dialogue often describe what the art depicts. This method of communication probably stems from an earlier time when comic books were aimed at younger readers. In order for those younger, less experienced readers to understand the story, clarity was emphasized. As audiences have evolved, more complex storytelling with less exposition heavy text treatment has developed.

In interviews, Windsor-Smith said that part of the reason he did *Weapon X* is because it took place outside of continuity. Because Wolverine's past was unknown, it was a blank slate for him to create the kind of story he wanted to write and draw without worrying about continuity or trying to read a bunch of comic books that he had no interest in reading.

> "If I had to do Marvel continuity, then I wouldn't be working for Marvel," [Windsor-Smith] says with amiable unconcern. "I don't read those books, anyway. And I don't care whether Wolverine's claws are supposed to be metal or shiny. I just did it. My attitude is that if you don't like it, you can't have it." (*Comics Scene* 18, p. 25)

Ultimately, Windsor-Smith was one of Marvel's most popular creators and Wolverine was one of their most popular characters. And there was a history of success between the creator, character, and editor, so *Weapon X* was greenlit.

6
Storytelling

Barry Windsor-Smith was one of the most popular creators at Marvel Comics. Part of his popularity was due to his style. His comics did not look like or read like other comic books. It is important to clarify that Windsor-Smith's style was not defined exclusively by his artwork. Windsor-Smith approached storytelling very differently than the standard Marvel house style approach.

The average age of comic book readers in the 1960s was 7. The storytelling style of Marvel as well as many other comic book publishers was "show and tell." Captions often described the drawing in the panel. This redundancy made sense for young, inexperienced readers. But by 1991, readers were older and hopefully better readers.

The 1980s saw the rise of creators who felt that comics were an art form and were not inherently limited to young readers. These creators challenged misconceptions about comics being for kids with complex, sophisticated works like *Maus*, *Watchmen*, *The Dark Knight Returns*, and *Love and Rockets*. The growth of storytelling in the art form meant that creators like Barry Windsor-Smith could use different techniques to engage and challenge their readers.

One of the more obvious storytelling choices in *Weapon X* is the lack of narrative captions. Without literal explanations, readers must pay close attention to Smith's artwork in each panel to follow *Weapon X*'s story. This one choice dramatically changes the reading experience. It places much more value on the artwork. One cannot understand the story only by reading the words. The art in each panel provides critical information. In order to understand what is happening, the reader must interpret the images and the character's dialogue. This was a radical departure from most Marvel comics of 1991. This kind of reading requires time, attention, and thought in order to process what we see and how it fits with other panels. It also creates an experience where the reader's knowledge is similar to Logan's—limited. We do not always know what is happening. We often piece together the story from a subjective, fragmented vantage point. At times, this effect makes Logan's character more relatable.

The complexity of this style of storytelling can only be achieved when the creative team is working in complete concert. That is hard to achieve in collaborations like film, television, and the Marvel method. But it is possible when one person is writing and drawing the story at the same time because the artist knows exactly what the writer is trying to say since they share a brain. Windsor-Smith's storytelling shifted the typical narrative responsibility of text onto the imagery, inverting the usual comic book reading experience. The result is an unusual reading experience, especially for a Marvel comic book.

The words that do exist in *Weapon X* are mostly dialogue spoken between the Professor, Dr. Cornelius, and Hines. Often these characters are not in the panel even though their words are. A lot of *Weapon X* features panels of Weapon X under observation. Juxtaposed on top of these images is dialogue from off-panel characters. Windsor-Smith uses color to designate which character is speaking. Windsor-Smith also cuts this dialogue into smaller pieces, sometimes causing dialogue to overlap other dialogue, as if the speakers are excitedly talking over one another. The placement of the word balloons does not always follow the left-to-right, top-to-bottom arrangement of Western reading conventions. This creates a disorienting effect and when coupled with the visuals makes for a narrative experience that challenges the reader to keep up and to acknowledge that what Logan is experiencing is horrific and that we do not know everything that is happening. It is unsettling and compliments the tone of the story. For most of this story, there are no answers. Even the main characters seem unsure of what is going on at times, who is ultimately behind this experiment, and whether they should be doing what they are doing. Look at that last sentence and try to think of another Marvel comic with that much uncertainty and moral ambiguity.

> "...this isn't spelled out," Windsor-Smith adds, "...where they've got all these explanatory thought balloons. If you don't pick up from whatever action's on the page, you're not going to pick it up."
>
> "The storytelling is very conventional," he notes. "It's just the way I normally do stuff. But the attitude is non-Marvel. I don't like that 'reveal everything' thing that Marvel has been doing for 25 years." (*Comics Scene* 18, April 1991, p. 24)

The eight-page installments of *Marvel Comics Presents* contrasted with the 20–22 pages of the standard Marvel comic books of that time. Windsor-Smith creates lean, effective chapters that advance the story and often jump ahead in time from chapter to chapter. The amount of time between chapters is not always clear. This adds to Logan's suffering because it makes the experiment feel like it carries on and on. And it feels like we only see the highlights in *Weapon X*, the tip of the Experiment-X iceberg.

The treatment of the character Logan is another bold choice. He spends most of the story drugged out of his mind. Chapters pass without any expression of agency from the character. The trauma and drugs put him in a zombie-like state, a supporting character in his own origin story.

Helpless.

Comics Scene magazine summed it up: "the true character of Wolverine is not much on display" (*Comics Scene* 18, April 1991, p. 24).

Windsor-Smith's extensive use of cross-cutting in early chapters is another example of storytelling that is not typical of Marvel Comics in 1991 or today. Windsor-Smith uses this technique to establish multiple sets of characters before they all converge. He also cuts through time. Panels jump forward and backward in time. Dreams, memories, programming…it is not always clear what we're seeing and how we should interpret it. At one point, Weapon X kills his experimenters, only for them to reappear in the subsequent chapter alive and well. It is later revealed that Weapon X was misled to believe that he had killed them as part of the mental manipulation of the program. But the reading experience is somewhat confusing as it seems like time is not unfolding in a natural, linear manner. All of this creates a feeling or sense similar to what Logan is experiencing—what exactly is happening? What is real? It all serves to create a memorable read that invites rereading.

The only similar Marvel comic that I can compare it to is Frank Miller and Bill Sienkiewicz's *Elektra: Assassin*—another story that features unconventional storytelling techniques that seem to mirror the distorted perception of its characters.

According to interviews with Barry Windsor-Smith, he created several of the *Weapon X* chapters out of sequence. The effect is that chapters vary from linear cliffhanger stories to fragments and scenes that change the tempo and tone of the story. This approach was chosen because it is how Windsor-Smith wanted to work on the story.

> It's kind of hard to describe. It's such a meandering process that I've put this thing together with. It's a tight story now, but the way it started out was, to be kind, let's say uni-directional. There are some stories in there that are typed eight-pagers. They start on page one and end hard on page eight. And two-thirds of the way through the series the action started to move so fast, and this was basically out of my control. I just do what the characters seem to want to do naturally because I don't like all of that real forced character stuff. So I just let it run. And it then became a serial in that there's a cliffhanger suddenly, and then there's another cliffhanger. Like I say, none of this is planned. I just did what seemed natural. (*Amazing Heroes* 188, February 1991, p. 32)

This approach compliments the story. *Weapon X* is a cross between slasher body horror and psychological thriller. By making the chapters of *Weapon X* feel like incomplete fragments that are missing bits of information, the story is unsettling. The audience struggles to make certain pieces fit together and it forces the audience to contemplate some details that push the darkness further than one would expect a super hero story to go. Like Logan, readers are never on firm ground. The more story we get, the less certain any of it seems.

In several chapters, they test Weapon X. Then the team analyzes the results and what to do next in their quest to perfect their killing machine. The next chapter often features the upgrade while the audience is left to imagine the time and procedure(s) that Logan has undergone. These upgrades often mean greater control over Weapon X's body and agency. They continue to erase or destroy his mind. In some chapters he is catatonic when "turned off," as requested by the Professor. The duration of Experiment-X is not revealed. It seems to exist outside of the real world. Inside the facility, the lack of day and night further destroys the integrity of time and rhythm of one's life. How long is Logan drugged and experimented on? What kind of torture and drugs destroys one's id? What will he remember if he ever regains autonomy? Great horror stories often imply the worst horror rather than show it. The horror is set up but the execution takes place in the dark recesses of the audience's minds. The way Windsor-Smith tells the story of *Weapon X*, the audience must fill in information based on the content that is shown. It is a brilliant use of storytelling and closure. It makes a disturbing story like *Weapon X* unforgettable because part of it takes place in the mind of each reader. The ability to create disturbing horror in comics is not easy. This kind of storytelling elevates *Weapon X* above and beyond Windsor-Smith's extraordinary artwork.

7

Violence

Wolverine is a killer. He is also one of Marvel's most popular intellectual properties. One could argue that Wolverine's popularity is based on his violent behavior. Any writer will tell you that character is defined by action. So if being a killer is a (the?) defining part of his character, then Wolverine's origin must address this characteristic.

Weapon X is the most violent comic story that Marvel ever published. There are stories with higher body counts but in terms of graphic horror and torture, Windsor-Smith's *Weapon X* knows no peer. What pushes it over the top is the combination of physical and psychological devastation wrought against Logan.

The Professor's goal with Experiment-X is to create "the most formidable tactical weapon ever conceived." The person or people behind the experiment must be able to control Weapon X the way someone controls a gun, a tank, or a drone. Weapon

X cannot possess free will. In addition to extreme physical modification that is only possible due to his mutant healing factor, Logan's mind must also be destroyed so that he can be manipulated like a machine, or more precisely, like a weapon.

The entity behind Experiment-X identifies Logan as a good subject. Some of the participants are led to believe that this is based on certain antisocial characteristics and his military history but that facade falls away as the experiment progresses.

Using violent force, the mysterious agents of Experiment-X subdue and abduct him. Early in the experimental process, the team learns that Logan is a mutant. As the experiment veers into more and more disturbing territory, it becomes apparent that his mutant healing ability is critical to survive the barbaric process of bonding adamantium to his skeleton. Lest anyone doubt his mad scientist villainy, the Professor makes it clear to his subordinates—Logan is a mutant, less than human, and therefore not worthy of sympathy or basic human rights. This is a blatant act of dehumanization. Dehumanization is the denial of full humanity in others along with the cruelty and suffering that accompany it. This theme is part of the X-Men, humans versus mutants. But *Weapon X* pushes it to graphic and horrific heights. In the context of human experimentation, the first thing that came to my mind was Nazi Germany. Windsor-Smith's subsequent graphic novel *Monsters* (2023, Fantagraphics) also features Nazi experiments. In *Amazing*

Heroes 188, while promoting *Weapon X*, Windsor-Smith revealed that he was working on the *Monsters* graphic novel so it is not difficult to connect these themes to *Weapon X*. It certainly adds to the story's darkness.

Examples of dehumanization occur again and again throughout *Weapon X*. In chapter five, there is a field test where Weapon X is placed in the Canadian winter wilderness with freezing and snowy conditions. He is naked, except for the devices that enable the Professor to control him. In the harsh climate, wolves attack Weapon X. The wolves have not been fed for six days in order to make sure that they are desperate and hungry for flesh. Weapon X responds to the vicious assault and kills the wolves with his claws, delighting the Professor.

His mood turns to disappointment when informed that there are no more wolves available for Weapon X to kill. He calls the handlers back to the compound after commanding them to leave Weapon X in the gory, sub-zero wilderness overnight. The only reason for this act is to continue the process of destroying Logan's humanity.

Weapon X references another historical atrocity—the CIA's MK-Ultra program. This program experimented on virtually everyone—students, hospital patients, prisoners, soldiers, civilians, even unwitting CIA agents. It destroyed countless lives—from Ted Kazinski, the Unabomber, who was exposed to psychological experiments connected to the MK-Ultra program as a college student at Harvard, to the CIA's own biological warfare scientist Frank Olson, who allegedly committed suicide while under the influence of LSD (see Errol Morris' 2017 documentary *Wormwood* for more details). Speculation also links Jack Ruby, Charles Manson, and many others to this project. MK-Ultra arose during the Cold War. When American POWs in the Korean War appeared to disavow their country, the United States, and specifically the CIA, responded by trying to create their own Manchurian candidates to combat the Reds. Barry Windsor-Smith was living in New York City when the *New York Times* covered this sensational story. The content of *Weapon X* suggests it was a major influence—a secret organization (presumably military) uses drugs and torture to try to create a perfect killing machine. It is almost literally the story of MK-Ultra. Although Windsor-Smith does not explicitly name the CIA or any organization or country behind Weapon X, Marvel Comics canon eventually does link the CIA and the Canadian government to the program.

> A decade ago Logan was captured and subjected to experiments by the Weapon X Project, a covert operation based in Canada that was jointly run by the CIA and the Canadian government. (*Essential Wolverine* 3, October 2000, p. 526)

In terms of violence, every chapter offers some. Often it is physical but almost equally, it is psychological. From minor aggressions like dumping coffee on a passed-out Logan's face after he has been turned off to overt acts of cruelty like leaving him in freezing cold conditions covered in the blood of dead wolves.

The Professor's disregard for human life occurs early in the story when a young, inexperienced tech is left alone with Weapon X. The Professor's decision leads to the young man's death. The Professor's reaction is one of pride, an early success in the "experiment."

As the scientists shape Weapon X into a tactical weapon, he

cuts guards to pieces, he cuts the Professor's hands off, and he seems to fantasize about killing various people—or perhaps it is another example of Windsor-Smith's manipulation of time, as these are actually events that will occur as the story unfolds. In trials, Weapon X kills wolves, a bear, and a tiger. The Professor uses Hines as bait, throwing her in harm's way, but careful not to break her neck so she can scream and draw Weapon X's attention. Before the story even begins, Logan's files reveal he killed someone at the gun range and Dr. Cornelius is on the run from the law due to patient-assisted suicides.

In the end, the mysterious person or group behind Experiment-X sacrifices the entire team. Is that part of the plan all along or is it a result of Logan's mutant healing power and strong will? Like much of *Weapon X*, it is not completely clear.

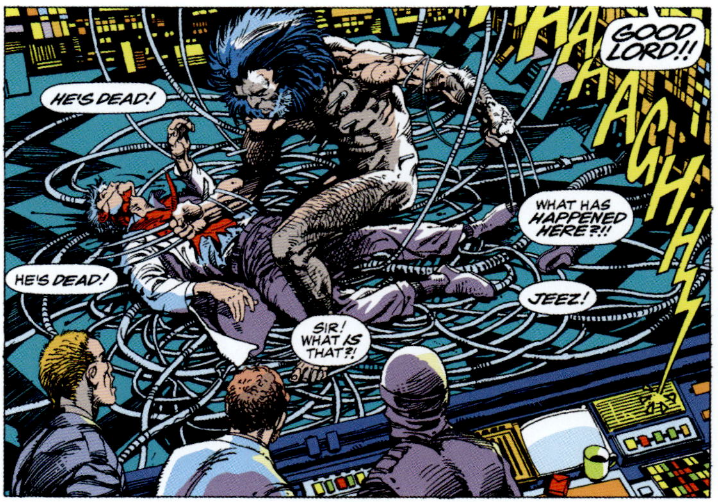

But what we do see is a lot of blood and a man who has been stripped of his clothing and dignity, a man who spends most of the book grunting and screaming in pain unable to summon the language to beg for help or mercy.

Marvel comics of the late 1980s and early 1990s were full of violence. The Punisher had three monthly books and killed hundreds of people over the course of those long-running titles. The demonic vigilante Ghost Rider chained up victims and dragged them behind his motorcycle as penance for their sins. Comic books are full of assassins, ninjas, barbarians, and vigilantes, but they rarely focus on the traumatic receipts of the violence. And that is what separates *Weapon X*. To see a favorite character reduced to a state of helplessness and subjected to gruesome experiments is not the same as the cartoony violence of *Looney Tunes* or Arnold Schwarzenegger movies full of witty one-liners. This is not throwing a knife through someone and telling them to "stick around." It is the ultimate inversion of the male super hero fantasy. Helplessness.

The origin of Wolverine is dark and violent. To truly be his origin it had to traumatize Logan enough that his superhuman healing factor could never fully repair or undo the damage that he suffered. It destroyed the line between his humanity and animalistic instincts—something the character continues to struggle with to this day.

8

Animals, Monsters, and Men

When Barry Windsor-Smith wrote and drew *Weapon X*, Wolverine's past was a mystery. The character was popular because Chris Claremont had developed him in *X-Men* and in the *Wolverine* limited series (with collaborator and superstar artist Frank Miller). What was known about the character was based on his present day exploits. He possessed an animalistic nature. He displayed a heightened sense of smell like a bloodhound. He had no moral problem with killing, much like a wild animal. When provoked or hurt, he often lost control of himself, his humanity disappeared, and he reverted to a savage beast-like state. This berserker element of Wolverine was so well known that Claremont's and Miller's collaboration on a *Wolverine* limited series focused on Logan's attempts through martial arts training and discipline to control his inner animalistic rage.

In *Weapon X*, Logan spends most of the story looking and acting like a wounded animal or a bloodthirsty monster rather than a human being. Comparisons to Frankenstein's monster seem clear, from the laboratory setting to the inhuman experimentation that he endures to people's reaction to Logan as Experiment-X unfolds.

In 2021, Fantagraphics published Barry Windsor-Smith's graphic novel *Monsters*. Windsor-Smith had worked on this story for 35 years. It began as a story for *The Incredible Hulk* comic book. Disagreement with editorial led to Windsor-Smith developing the story on his own. A theme of *Monsters* is abuse and the traumatic effects of abuse on the survivor's life. Windsor-Smith began working on this story before *Weapon X* and continued doing so for decades afterwards. Thematically, there are some parallels. The idea of trauma as an origin or catalyst for a character is in both. Unlike Peter Parker receiving spider-like powers from a radioactive spider bite or the Fantastic Four being exposed to radiation, Windsor-Smith uses something much darker to create Wolverine—trauma.

Besides killing people, Weapon X faces several animals in field trials. The scientists watch these trials on monitors from the safety and comfort of their lab. The contrast between the wilderness setting and the controlled laboratory makes Weapon X feel more animal than human from a physical standpoint. The human scientists are inside while the animals are outside.

And the battles between Weapon X and the animals resemble savage, monster fights like old Saturday matinees or Japanese kaiju movies. But the context of the story creates the opposite effect. As the scientists watch these violent spectacles, they appear to be the real monsters in the story. They engineered this experiment. They are trying to turn Logan into a living weapon. They view his violent actions with varying degrees of self-satisfaction for a job well done.

What about the audience? What is the role of the consumers who made Weapon X the most popular story in the 187-issue history of *Marvel Comics Presents*? Critics often view art as a reflection of society. If art is a valid mirror for society, then what does a super hero like Wolverine say about the society that celebrates him?

Considering Wolverine's popularity as a second-generation Marvel super hero, is it reasonable to consider how the character reflects the changing zeitgeist of American society. One of the qualities of the super hero genre is how the super hero fantasy reflects and comments on the society and culture that reads it. The original Marvel Universe was created in the early 1960s, a vestige of the greatest generation—Jack Kirby, Steve Ditko, and Stan Lee were all army veterans from the 1940s. Spider-Man, Fantastic Four, and the Avengers were heroes in a traditional moralistic sense. But Wolverine was created over a decade later. The Cold War raged, the Civil

Rights Movement and Vietnam War divided the country and exposed ugly, inhumane treatment of Americans by their fellow Americans, Nixon resigned in shame, the economy was the worst it had been since the Great Depression, and the CIA was trying to control the minds of the American people! Logan was not the only one subjected to violent changes at the time. American society had endured its own extreme culture shocks.

By the late 1980s and early 1990s, platforms like *Rolling Stone* magazine published articles declaring that the super hero was all grown up. So what does this postmodern super hero reveal about us? Like the scientists, the readers are watching this sadistic story and following the traumatic mistreatment of their favorite character. Weapon X sold well. *Marvel Comics Presents* sales increased with the serialization of this story. Had the comic book audience become monsters by 1991? Instead of do-gooder heroes saving the day, did readers want to see the heroes tortured and suffering? According to their wallets, that's exactly what they wanted.

I can only speculate why, but one thing is clear—the times were changing. Comics weren't just for kids anymore.

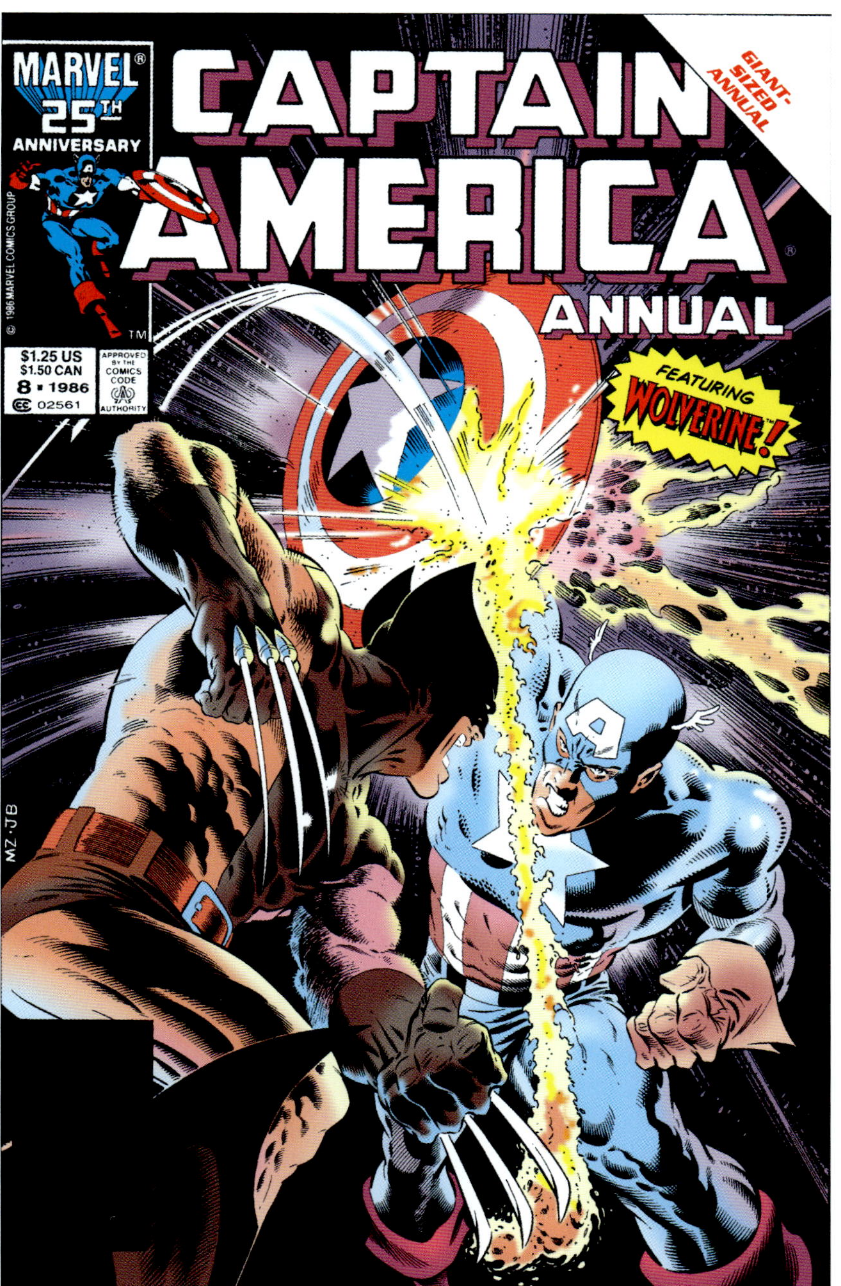
MARVEL
25TH
ANNIVERSARY
© 1986 MARVEL COMICS GROUP
CAPTAIN AMERICA
ANNUAL
GIANT-SIZED ANNUAL
$1.25 US
$1.50 CAN
8 • 1986
02561
APPROVED BY THE COMICS CODE AUTHORITY
FEATURING
WOLVERINE!
MZ·JB

9

1960s in the 1990s: The Setting of WEAPON X

There are two temporal settings for *Weapon X*. There is the time when *Weapon X* was published, 1991, and there is the time when the story is set.

In real life, 1991 is a fascinating time period in American comics. This era is known as the speculator boom and one could argue that 1991 is its peak based on the record sales of Rob Liefeld's *X-Force* 1 (5 million copies) and Jim Lee's *X-Men* 1 (8 million copies).

While speculators were buying comic books in big numbers, another trend at this time was "grim and gritty" super heroes. Creators like Alan Moore, Dave Gibbons, and Frank Miller had achieved massive critical and commercial success with dark, revisionist interpretations of super heroes in *Watchmen* and *Dark Knight Returns.* Comic books have always chased trends. So these hits from the late 1980s inspired creators and publishers towards darker, more violent comic books and characters. The Punisher is a serial killer/mass murderer/vigilante who kills criminals. He was a very popular Marvel character and starred in three monthly books in the 1990s. With sales through the roof, violent heroes and antiheroes seemed like an unbeatable formula in the early 1990s. In that context, *Weapon X* fits perfectly.

To be clear, for anyone unfamiliar with the speculator boom of the early 1990s, it went bust like all bubbles do. By the late 1990s, comic book sales shrunk by almost 90 percent. Most comic book distributors went out of business. In the early 1990s there were almost 20 distributors; by the end of the 1990s, there was only one. Marvel Comics declared bankruptcy in 1996. Boom and bust. Also noteworthy, the trend of violent, "adult" comics would also reverse. Today, the second most successful publisher of comics and graphic novels is Scholastic, known for their all-ages titles. Viz is the number one publisher of comics and graphic novels. Their output is primarily manga (Japanese comics). But I digress…

It is also possible to view *Weapon X* through the lens of revisionist super heroes. Frank Miller tackled the Golden Age with his reinterpretation of Batman. Moore and Gibbons deconstructed the Silver Age when they dissected avatars of the Charlton heroes in *Watchmen*. Windsor-Smith's take on Wolverine can be considered in the same postmodern context but applied to the Bronze Age of American comics. The Golden Age covers the first wave of comic books, up to the 1954 Senate hearings and the subsequent rise of the Comics Code Authority. The Silver Age started in 1956 when DC Comics brought the Flash back and super heroes began to rise in popularity. The end of the Silver Age is less clear, sometime in the early 1970s, perhaps when Denny O'Neil and Neal Adams took over *Green Lantern/Green Arrow* and did a series of stories about the socio-economic conditions of the time. Others say the Silver Age ended when Spider-Man failed to save Gwen Stacy. Her death signaled the end of the innocence of the Silver Age. Jack Kirby, one of the major architects of the Marvel Universe, left Marvel in 1970 and went to DC Comics. Another possible marker for the Silver Age's end. Some comics historians say the biggest event of the Silver Age is the rise of underground comix—noteworthy because they are typically the work of one cartoonist who handles all of the writing and art and they were completely unregulated by the Comics Code. The underground comix tackled adult subject matter and were read by adults. The Bronze Age followed the Silver Age. The Bronze Age features darker plot elements and storylines more related to relevant social issues. Comic book stores and the direct market came to prominence during the Bronze Age. Wolverine, the Punisher, and the Teenage Mutant Ninja Turtles were introduced during the Bronze Age. It runs from around 1970–1985.

The time period when *Weapon X* takes place is not clearly defined. This is common for super hero origin stories. After all, no one wants to read a comic book about a man in his late nineties dressing up as a bat (actually, if Batman was 25 in 1939, he'd be over 100 now). To avoid this awkward aging issue, super hero stories are intentionally vague when it comes to specific dates, especially for origins. As I have noted earlier, Windsor-Smith does not give a precise timeline for *Weapon X*, only saying that it is set some time in the earlier 1960s (*Amazing Heroes* 188, February 1991, p. 31)—a time of deep political unrest and uncertainty in American history.

The early 1960s was also the dawn of the Marvel Universe. The comic book industry had suffered its own major downturn after the Senate subcommittee hearings on juvenile delinquency of 1954. Comic book sales plummeted in the aftermath. Publishers went out of business. Professionals left the field. Marvel was on the brink of shutting down their comics line. But one last effort from Jack Kirby and Stan Lee turned everything around. First came *The Fantastic Four* and soon the Marvel Universe followed.

By the end of the 1960s, business was booming at Marvel Comics—and they needed to add more talent. Windsor-Smith's comic book career began at Marvel in 1968 and saw him rise to fan-favorite in the 1970s off the strength of his work on *Conan the Barbarian*. The turmoil of the 1960s must have made an impression on Windsor-Smith. The themes of *Weapon X* fit that tumultuous time period like a glove—paranoia, mistrust of authority, violence, corruption, drugs! These are the main ingredients of *Weapon X*.

It is quite a coincidence that while the Marvel Universe was blossoming in the early 1960s, one of their most popular characters was abducted and experimented on in a sinister, para-military intelligence project.

The location settings of *Weapon X* are limited to three spaces: the Prophecy, the Experiment-X facility, and the wintery Canadian wilderness.

The Prophecy is a rundown hotel for fallen Christians. Logan lies about his faith in order to get a room there. The Prophecy only appears in the prologue. The name seems to be the most important part. "Prophecy is part of the apocalypse. Didja know that?"

Wires fill the Experiment-X facility and it resembles a 1970s sci-fi film set crossed with Stanley Kubrick's *2001* (1968). The design features a lot of black ink, broken up with colorful, saturated rectangles and circles. It's a black light poster—perhaps a design reference to the 1960s/70s psychedelic culture and underground comix of the period setting. As a four-color

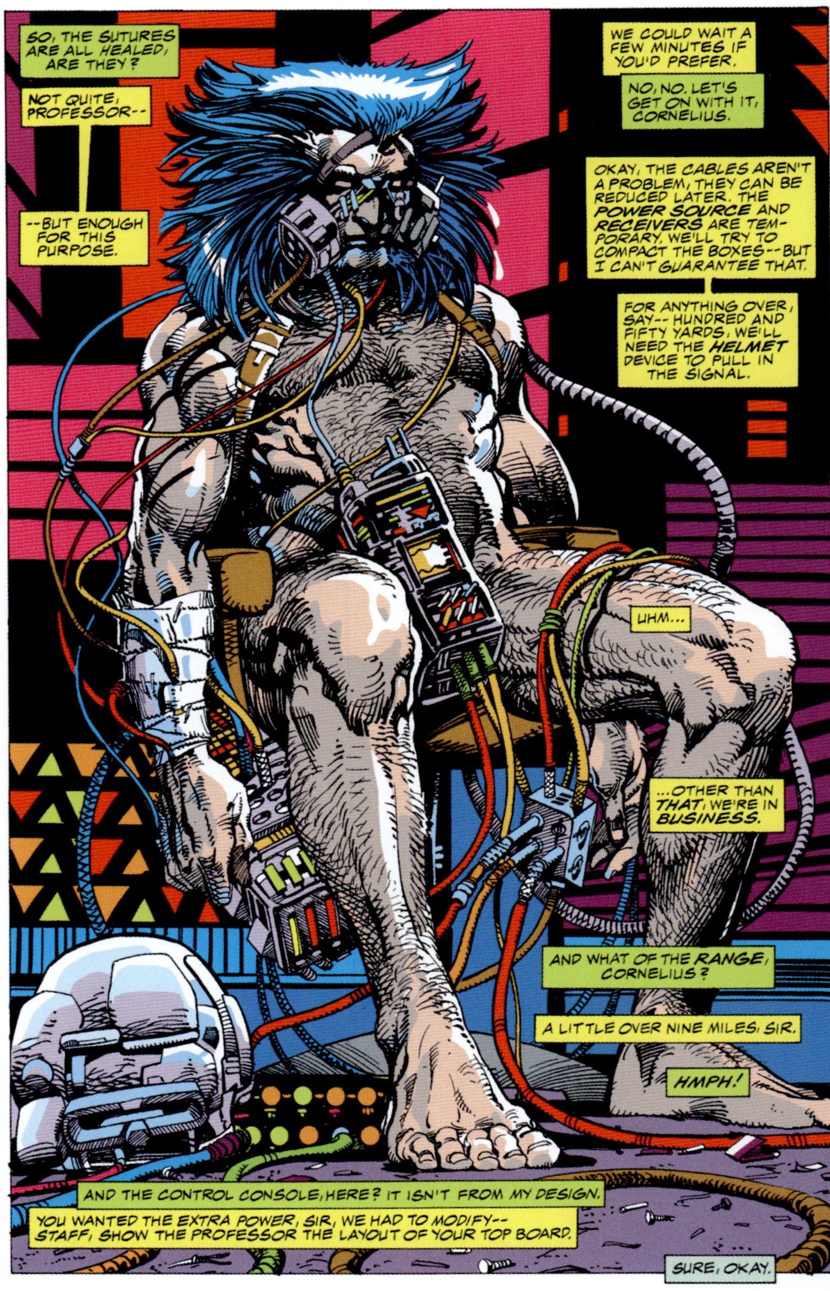
SO, THE SUTURES ARE ALL HEALED, ARE THEY?
NOT QUITE, PROFESSOR--
--BUT ENOUGH FOR THIS PURPOSE.
WE COULD WAIT A FEW MINUTES IF YOU'D PREFER.
NO, NO, LET'S GET ON WITH IT, CORNELIUS.
OKAY, THE CABLES AREN'T A PROBLEM, THEY CAN BE REDUCED LATER. THE POWER SOURCE AND RECEIVERS ARE TEMPORARY. WE'LL TRY TO COMPACT THE BOXES--BUT I CAN'T GUARANTEE THAT.
FOR ANYTHING OVER, SAY-- HUNDRED AND FIFTY YARDS, WE'LL NEED THE HELMET DEVICE TO PULL IN THE SIGNAL.
UHM...
...OTHER THAN THAT, WE'RE IN BUSINESS.
AND WHAT OF THE RANGE, CORNELIUS?
A LITTLE OVER NINE MILES, SIR.
HMPH!
AND THE CONTROL CONSOLE, HERE? IT ISN'T FROM MY DESIGN.
YOU WANTED THE EXTRA POWER, SIR, WE HAD TO MODIFY--
STAFF, SHOW THE PROFESSOR THE LAYOUT OF YOUR TOP BOARD.
SURE, OKAY.

comic book backdrop, it is beautiful. The hard edges of the background shapes contrast against the naked, organic flesh of Weapon X. The sharp edges of the architecture also make the facility feel cold and emphasize the inhumanity of the space. It looks like an uncomfortable, even painful space for a human body to rest or be imprisoned. It makes for a great update to the classic mad scientist laboratory, where computers, probes, and IVs have replaced beakers and Bunsen burners.

The dark hallways and generic architecture create a labyrinth and calls to mind another Kubrick movie, *The Shining*. Many words have been written about the impossibility of the Overlook Hotel's architecture in *The Shining*. The Experiment-X facility could share an architect with the disjunctive design and spatial uneasiness of Kubrick's horror masterpiece. This bizarre space adds tension and suspense to *Weapon X*. It is a perfect representation of Logan's tortured plight. He is a lab rat in a nightmarish military-industrial Kafkaesque maze. Comparisons to Kubrick's detail-oriented films are not unwarranted. Both men were known for an extreme level of control over their storytelling. Kubrick obsessed over details big and small with his team of collaborators. Meanwhile, Windsor-Smith took on more and more of the assembly line roles of the comic book factory until he was performing every task himself. Auteur is a film term, but if it applied to other forms of visual storytelling, it would suit Windsor-Smith's work here.

The brutalist architecture also contrasts against nature. Not that nature is welcoming in *Weapon X*. When it is time to test Weapon X, wranglers lead him into sub-zero, snow-covered wilderness. The straight lines of the facility give way to the harsh, organic conditions of the Canadian winter. The palette opens up, but it doesn't warm up. The Canadian winter is dark. The colors are cold blues and purples. We never see the sun, although the white snow provides a welcome break from the black interiors. Weapon X has several field tests, like a maximum security prisoner given a brief reprieve from his cell.

Even when Weapon X appears to escape at the end, there is little respite from the suffering. Logan, Weapon X, or perhaps he is now Wolverine, walks away from the compound. Still naked. The snow quickly covers his body and I wonder what continuous frostbite must feel like for someone with a healing factor.

Everything in this book screams pain. And everything is drawn beautifully. As Weapon X walks off into the snowy mountains, the Northern Lights appear overhead. They are an unexpected detail in the twilight of Weapon X's horrible experience. One more visual detail that adds to the subtle complexity of *Weapon X*.

The two main settings are another story choice that feels perfect. Both settings make sense for the character. They offer a binary variation like night and day. Lab work, then field trial, and repeat. The three field tests that appear in Weapon X follow Bushmiller's classic cartooning rule of three—one rock, two rocks, and a bunch of rocks. Suggesting a lot more than just three tests. I am not sure that the passage of time is considered "setting," but the surreal, dreamy depiction of time's passage in *Weapon X* contributes to the overall dystopian nightmare of the story. How long does Experiment-X go on?

Like the lean characterizations in the story, Smith wastes nothing. These two main settings are all that *Weapon X* needs. Inside, outside. Nature, science. Animal, man. The 1960s, the 1990s.

10

Color + Lettering

One of the most striking features of *Weapon X* is its color. Barry Windsor-Smith colored *Weapon X* himself. Like his line art, his coloring is stylistic and unique.

Coloring in comic books has changed dramatically since 1991. The primary difference is that today's comics are colored digitally and software generates color separations for the printing process. Digital coloring rose to prominence in the 1990s. Before that, colorists would paint and code color guides over photocopies of line art. Then people would create physical color separations by hand for printing. The color separations were limited to 0, 25, 50, or 100 percent of the ink colors cyan, magenta, and yellow. Fine dot patterns were used for 25 percent or 50 percent coverage. These inks could also be printed on top of each other to create the appearance of additional colors. For example, Caucasian skin was 25 percent magenta and 25 percent yellow. Marvel's color palette was 64 colors. The best examples of comic book coloring that use the 64-color palette are *Batman* issues 404–407 (colorist Richmond Lewis applied her painter's sense of color to the 64-color palette, then she actually painted the *Batman: Year One* collected colors so those do not feature the original 64-color palette treatment—it's a great chance to compare the differences between comic book coloring and full-color reproduction), *Watchmen* (colorist John Higgins emphasized secondary colors rather than the traditional super hero primary colors), and *Weapon X*.

Most comic books were printed on newsprint in 1991. Newsprint was very porous so the inks would lose some of their saturation as they were absorbed in the grayish, yellowish newsprint. Good colorists understood this and adjusted their

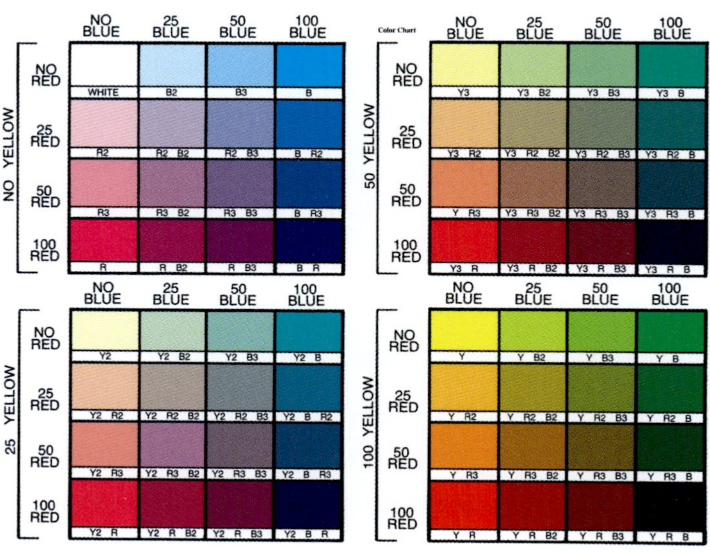

color for newsprint paper. Basically, bright colors would be less bright and the yellowish paper would unify the various colors, like a base color on a painted canvas.

Color is obviously important to Windsor-Smith. He colored several comics before and after *Weapon X*. His time running Gorblimey Press taught him a lot about color and reproduction. He also spent time painting and studying fine art while he was away from comics for twelve years.

Windsor-Smith's color work on *Weapon X* looks different to any other comic book I have ever seen. Most comics before digital coloring featured flat colors. There are a number of reasons for this. It is faster to cut out flat areas of color, so it is less expensive. Time is money. Comic books were very cheaply printed for most of their history. The printing and supplies led to bad registration and uneven printing. So the solution was simple colors and heavy black lines to hide some of the printing flaws, like bad registration. Windsor-Smith approached color like a painter. Since he colored a lot of his line work, the color feels more integral to the final illustration. It appears to be part of the design and storytelling. This is not uncommon for cartoonists who write, draw, and color their own work. I often note color concepts in my scripts.

In the case of Windsor-Smith's *Weapon X*, the line art is very complex with thoughtful lighting, cross-hatching, and small details. His color continues this visually complex approach.

Rather than flat color, he often uses multiple colors to describe people's faces, folds in their clothes, textures, liquids, and other surfaces. At times, his use of multiple colors on the same surface or space resembles painting. A character's face might have four or five colors rather than the flat 25 percent magenta and 25 percent yellow. He uses white as a highlight to suggest three-dimensional form. It is a fundamentally different approach to comic book coloring than most colorists used at the time.

In order to achieve these effects, Windsor-Smith actually outlined the shapes on his color guides in pen so the separators understood exactly what he intended. This technique was bold and different. It allowed for a precision of color detail that would not be seen again until digital technology completely revolutionized the coloring process of comic books. The style still has not been repeated.

The dramatic effect of Windsor-Smith's technique anticipated the dominant role color has assumed in the decades since. Today, color is often the most prominent visual element of many comic books. I would argue that color has replaced line art and composition as the house style at Marvel Comics. In *Weapon X*, the color and line art work together to define form, volume, texture, and value. Today, it is common for color to do these things, but in 1991, most of this was handled exclusively with line. Color was treated more like an afterthought or lesser element.

Windsor-Smith also approached the color palette of *Weapon X* like a painter or visual storyteller. He understood how to use color to express feelings, to create atmosphere, to compliment the scene, and to enhance the mood. In other words, Windsor-Smith uses color to communicate more information to the reader. His colors do not simply describe what is there. Windsor-Smith uses color the same way he uses words and line art. In his inimitable style, color creates sensation and meaning. For a visceral story like *Weapon X*, it is essential that color contributes to the storytelling. It emphasizes Logan's naked, vulnerable state. It disorients the reader when he is drugged and experimented on. It adds impact to the story. Sometimes it clarifies the art and sometimes it obscures it depending on the needs of the story or scene.

Barry Windsor-Smith does the work of an entire creative team on *Weapon X*. The only part of the process that Windsor-Smith did not handle completely is lettering.

The lettering is credited "by Jim Novak and Barry Windsor-Smith."

> I did half the lettering. I've got a great letterer on the book. He's my favorite letterer and I asked for him specifically: Jim Novak, who I think is terrific. But I do all my own sound effects. I draw them and Jim just inks them, basically, unless I've really screwed one up, in which case I put in the script "Please improve" and he always does. (*Amazing Heroes* 188, April 1991, p. 33)

Jim Novak began lettering for Marvel Comics in 1975. He spent many years working in the Marvel bullpen as a letterer. For *Weapon X,* Novak handled the traditional comic book lettering chores—word balloons and captions, presumably panel borders as well. Windsor-Smith's contribution to lettering was sound effects and compositional placement of lettering.

A lot of caption style lettering begins in the top-left corner of a panel, using the panel borders as the edge of the caption box. The effect is that the caption feels separate from the art. But in *Weapon X*, most of the caption boxes are inset. This allows color and line art to wrap around the boxes, integrating them visually with the overall page design. By setting captions and word balloons inside the artwork, it makes the text part of the image and should be read with the art, rather than before or separate from the art. It is another creative choice that brings the text and images closer together.

The same thoughtfulness can be seen in the way the word balloons and text boxes are arranged throughout each panel and page. Typically, American comic books are read top-left to top-right, then next row, left-to-right. In *Weapon X*, the lettering is often arranged in a U-shape and consists of several balloons or boxes per panel. This is not a standard approach to letter balloon placement in Marvel Comics (or DC, Dark Horse, Image, etc.). This arrangement appears in some of Windsor-Smith's Valiant work on *Archer & Armstrong* (1992–1993), suggesting a sensibility to word balloon placement that is different from many other comic book makers. The purpose of this compositional approach to balloon and text box placement is not always obvious. It adds to the sense of oddness in the story. It is dreamlike at times, as if the sound is not happening the way the reader expects it to. If this was Windsor-Smith's intention, it is interesting to consider how composition impacts the perception of sound in a comic. However, it is hard to believe that this was the intent since it is repeated in other comics that Windsor-Smith created. So, if not a storytelling effect, what is the purpose? Windsor-Smith drew and co-wrote several issues of *X-Men* with writer Chris Claremont. Claremont's *X-Men* scripts featured a lot of text and relied on letterer Tom Orzechowski's creativity to fit words into oddly-shaped balloons that wrapped around characters in dense panels and pages. Perhaps Windsor-Smith's lettering was a visual approximation of this style. Eddie Campbell, a cartoonist and comics historian, has written about how the placement of lettering in comics defies the traditional top-bottom, left-right reading order. Instead, he suggests that the reading order in a comic panel is based on proximity. The order goes from one balloon or caption box to the next nearest balloon or caption box. With this order in mind, perhaps Smith arranged the lettering in *Weapon X* with the reader's eye movement the priority. The lettering placement may be designed as a directional device to lead the reader's eye through each panel, rather than the usual technique of captions at the top of the panel. In the traditional placement, one reads the caption, then looks at or "reads" the image. Then moves onto the next panel. In *Weapon X*, panels feature a dozen word balloons or more. The eye constantly moves from text to image in order to read everything. The result is a much different reading experience than a standard comic book.

Larry Hama, long-time Marvel editor and writer (and artist), wrote the introduction for the 1993 *Wolverine: Weapon X* collected edition. In his introduction, Hama describes Windsor-Smith's work on *Weapon X* as "such a seamless melding of writing and drawing that one cannot be separated from the other, and it is impossible to tell where one ends and the other

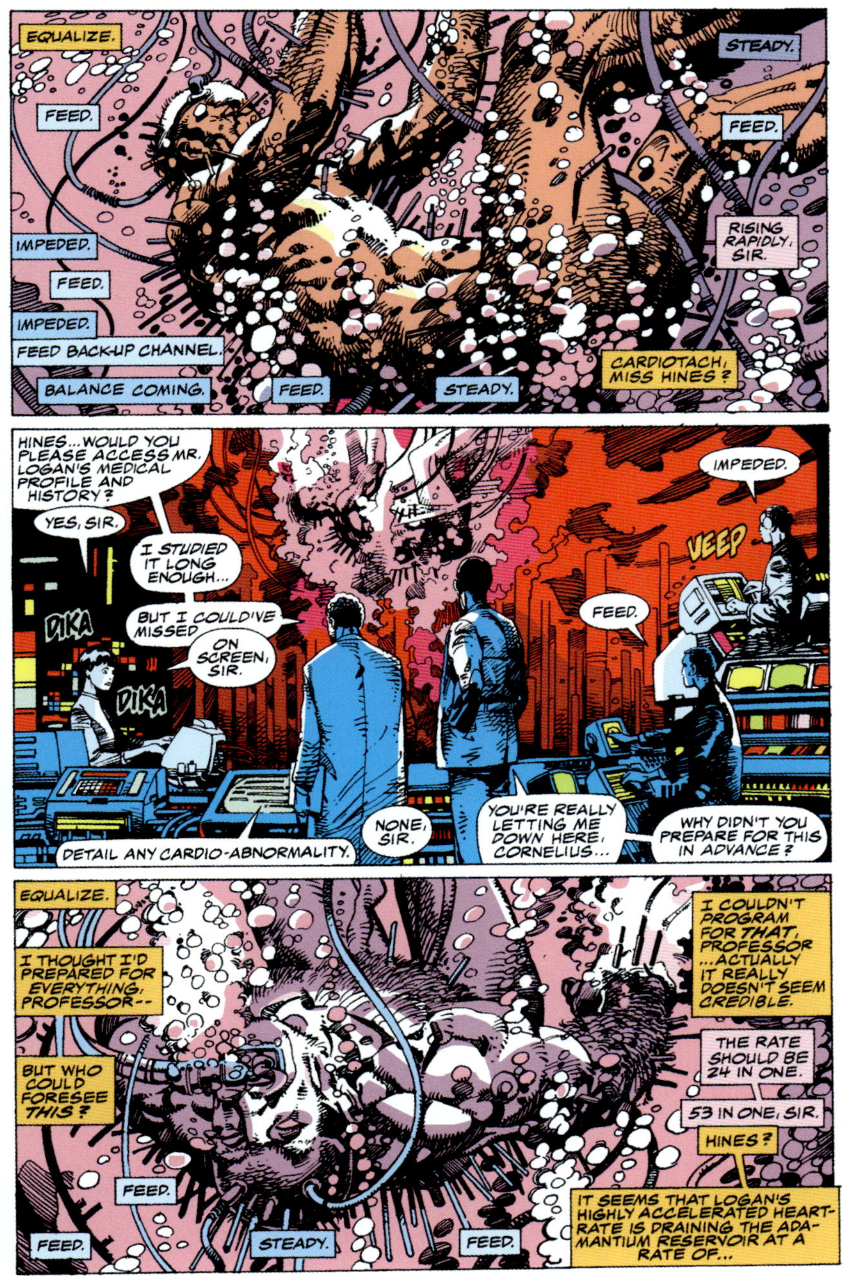
EQUALIZE.
FEED.
STEADY.
FEED.
IMPEDED.
FEED.
IMPEDED.
FEED BACK-UP CHANNEL.
RISING RAPIDLY, SIR.
BALANCE COMING.
FEED.
STEADY.
CARDIOTACH, MISS HINES?
HINES...WOULD YOU PLEASE ACCESS MR. LOGAN'S MEDICAL PROFILE AND HISTORY?
YES, SIR.
I STUDIED IT LONG ENOUGH...
BUT I COULD'VE MISSED
ON SCREEN, SIR.
DIKA
DIKA
IMPEDED.
VEEP
FEED.
DETAIL ANY CARDIO-ABNORMALITY.
NONE, SIR.
YOU'RE REALLY LETTING ME DOWN HERE, CORNELIUS...
WHY DIDN'T YOU PREPARE FOR THIS IN ADVANCE?
EQUALIZE.
I THOUGHT I'D PREPARED FOR EVERYTHING, PROFESSOR--
BUT WHO COULD FORESEE THIS?
I COULDN'T PROGRAM FOR THAT, PROFESSOR ...ACTUALLY IT REALLY DOESN'T SEEM CREDIBLE.
THE RATE SHOULD BE 24 IN ONE.
53 IN ONE, SIR.
HINES?
FEED.
FEED.
STEADY.
FEED.
IT SEEMS THAT LOGAN'S HIGHLY ACCELERATED HEART-RATE IS DRAINING THE ADAMANTIUM RESERVOIR AT A RATE OF...

picks up." This observation applies to *Weapon X*'s coloring and lettering. Each component of *Weapon X* fits together in a way that few comic books ever achieve.

11

Production + Process

The production and process of Weapon X may be what separates it the most from other Marvel comics. Every step of the creative process differed from the typical Marvel comic.

One of the more curious parts of Weapon X history is that it was done outside of the X-office. In the early 1990s, Marvel had group editors that oversaw related titles. Bob Harras was the editor of the X-titles—including *X-Men*, *Uncanny X-Men*, *X-Force*, *X-Factor*, and *Wolverine*. But he was not the editor of *Weapon X*. *Weapon X* was published in *Marvel Comics Presents*, a title that Terry Kavanagh edited.

Marvel Comics Presents was a bi-weekly comic book anthology. Each issue featured four stories. Each story was 8 pages compared to a standard Marvel comic book story that was 20–22 pages at the time. Wolverine was usually the lead feature because the character sold comic books.

The stories were not tied to continuity the way that most Marvel comic books were. This might be due to editorial as well as the title's unusual bi-weekly schedule. Since the book featured different characters in each issue, it did not fit into one editorial group like Bob Harras' X-office, for example. It was different from the typical Marvel comic.

Terry Kavanagh had been an assistant editor for the *X-Men* comic books. Windsor-Smith drew several X-Men stories, including *Uncanny X-Men* 186 and 198, *Lifedeath* 1 and 2, and *Uncanny X-Men* 205 featuring a violent Wolverine Christmas story. That experience, coupled with Windsor-Smith's popularity, led Kavanagh to ask Smith to do something for *Marvel Comics Presents.*

Since Wolverine's origin was a blank slate, or so he thought, Windsor-Smith could write a story without having to read a bunch of comic books or worry about making the story fit into a complex history.

The earliest mention of Barry Windsor-Smith's *Weapon X* appeared in the July 27, 1988 issue of *Comic Shop News*. The actual story was not published for over three years. Part of that is due to Barry Windsor-Smith handling most of the creative roles in the comic's production. He was also in a serious car accident and could not work for six months.

MARVEL®
THE UNCANNY
X-MEN
© 1985 MARVEL COMICS GROUP
TM
65¢
198
OCT
02461
APPROVED BY THE COMICS CODE AUTHORITY
LIFE-DEATH II
Claremont
&
Windsor-Smith

In *Comics Scene* magazine, he joked that Marvel let him do this story because they figured he'd never finish it!

> "I think the truth is that nobody at Marvel thought I was going to finish it," Windsor-Smith chuckles, "so they didn't want to say anything! Terry was stunned when I called him up and said, 'Well, that's it. It's done. What next?'" (*Comics Scene* 18, April 1991, p. 22)

Windsor-Smith created chapters out of sequence. A close examination of the story reveals artistic differences between chapters, even the way captions are positioned in panels varies between several chapters. It is an interesting way to create a comic. Todd McFarlane said that he would draw several pages, then lay them all out, and arrange them to make a story. Other creators have talked about drawing graphic novels out of sequence because they anticipate some style changes due to the length of time it takes to draw a graphic novel. By drawing a book out of sequence, these changes may seem less pronounced.

Windsor-Smith chose to work this way because "I didn't have a full plot when I started. I just had a couple of story ideas and a general concept, and I didn't want to hang around and figure out a whole story. I kind of like not knowing what I'm going to do next" (*Amazing Heroes* 188, April 1991, p. 32).

Combined with his interest in the eight-page format, the effect of this approach is that each eight-page chapter feels different but also complete and satisfying. The chapters are pieces of a bigger narrative, but they also deliver a short story with a beginning, middle, and end. Most of *Weapon X*'s chapters focus on an idea, a scene, or a theme. They read as distinct pieces of an epic. Like a chapter in a novel, these eight-page chapters advance the characters, raise the stakes, reveal information, ask questions, and invite the reader to return for more. While this may seem like obvious ingredients for serial storytelling, not all comic books deliver it. Creating chapters out of sequence may have been a way for Windsor-Smith to focus on the subject or idea that most excited him at the time. And it may have allowed the ideas that were not completely developed to continue to grow in his imagination. Write and draw the chapter that is ready and come back to the chapter that is not ready in the future after you've had more time to consider it.

The X-Office learned about *Weapon X* when Windsor-Smith started to bring chapters to Marvel. As editor of *Marvel Comics Presents*, Kavanagh had to coordinate stories with various editorial offices to ensure that characters were being used properly. When the early *Weapon X* chapters surfaced in the X-Office, there were some concerns. It turned out Chris Claremont, the long-time *X-Men* writer, had his own ideas about Wolverine's origin (a topic discussed in Chapter 3). After acknowledging Claremont's hurt feelings, Windsor-Smith added a few details in order to keep Claremont's idea viable.

Throughout the creative process of *Weapon X*, both Kavanagh and the X-Office editor, Bob Harras, signed off on each chapter.

The most challenging parts of Windsor-Smith's process were handling so much of the production himself and working without a complete plan for the story.

> It's kind of hard to describe. It's such a meandering process that I've put this together with. It's a tight story now, but the way it started out was, to be kind, let's say uni-directional. There are some stories in there that are typed eight-pagers. They start on page one and end hard on page eight. And two-thirds of the way through the series the action started to move so fast, and this was basically out of my control. I just do what the characters seem to want to do naturally because I don't like all of that real forced character stuff. So I just let it run. And it then became a serial in that there's a cliffhanger suddenly, and then there's another cliffhanger. Like I say, none of this is planned. I just did what seemed natural.
>
> I don't like everything being consistent. I like the art to look like how the artist and writer felt at the time. It's far

more invigorating than anything that's been pre-planned and has to look homogenized through the Marvel style. (*Amazing Heroes* 188, April 1991, pp. 32–33)

Windsor-Smith brought two advantages to *Weapon X* that are practically impossible for others to follow. First, as a single creator, he completely understands what he is trying to accomplish as a storyteller and he can use the writing, text, composition, line, value, color, and lettering to communicate his intent. No matter how close a collaborative team is, each member has their own mind and understanding of what they are trying to do. It is impossible for two people to think exactly the same way and to understand each other completely. Second, Windsor-Smith's robust skillset is virtually unparalleled. He was a successful comic book artist, then he left comics and spent twelve years studying art. When he returned to comic books, he brought a unique and unmatched set of skills and experience to the art form. It's worth noting that Windsor-Smith may have been the best romantic anatomist drawing American comics in 1991. Anatomy is a vital skill of a super hero comic artist and a defining trope of the genre. *Weapon X* allowed him to put this anatomical mastery to work as he showed in painstaking detail the torture and transformation of a human body into a weapon.

David Mazzucchelli is one of the most celebrated cartoonists in Marvel/DC history. After achieving enormous success with

Daredevil: Born Again and *Batman: Year One*, he left corporate comics and the super hero genre and went on to produce his own comics as a writer, penciller, inker, letterer, colorist, designer, and publisher. In *The Comics Journal* 152 (pages 115–116), he talked about a lesson that he learned early in his career when he was freelancing for Marvel on *Daredevil*.

> Whenever I had work to turn in, I brought it in person, because I took a real interest in what happened to it when it got out of my hands. I learned early on that the look of a book is determined by the last person who gets his hands on it. It was very important to me, if I was going to put my best effort into something, to try to see that it got to the printer in at least some kind of stage that I knew about. At least as far along as I could go. So I was usually in the office when pages were being turned in or I would always check the color before it went out. I had a lot of hand in how the covers were going to look after I had drawn the image. That, to me, is part of what I considered the job of being the artist on a book.

I cannot help but think of Mazzucchelli's words when I consider Windsor-Smith's role on *Weapon X*. By doing virtually every part of the creative process, Windsor-Smith ensured that he was the last person to get his hands on the book.

12
Legacy

Wolverine remains one of Marvel's most popular characters. His origin story, *Weapon X* as told by Windsor-Smith, has been mined for 35 years for other comic books and movies. An entire, multimedia universe has developed since the publication of *Weapon X* around the Weapon X Project.

While that continuity may be of interest to some, it is not reflective of Windsor-Smith's intention with the original story, although he did draw five pages of artwork for a flashback sequence from *Wolverine* 166 (written by Frank Tieri) that is set during *Weapon X*. Other popular characters have been connected to the Weapon X program, including Deadpool, Wolverine's long-time enemy Sabretooth, and X-23.

Windsor-Smith's *Weapon X* has become an indelible part of the Marvel Universe. Although it was mentioned in comics before Windsor-Smith chronicled this epic tale, it's hard to imagine it would be so iconic without his unique take.

Shortly after its initial publication, Marvel released hardcover and softcover editions of the collected story. This practice has become standard in American comics. But in the early 1990s, the "graphic novel" was not the standard publishing model at Marvel Comics. Comics that succeeded as perennial collections were still an emerging business model. *Weapon X*'s sustained success has made its publication history special.

In 2004, Marvel published a prose novel called *Wolverine: Weapon X*, authored by Marc Cerasini, a *New York Times* bestseller and prolific author of fiction and non-fiction. Marvel published a number of books based on their characters. The fact that *Weapon X*, a 13-year-old story (at that time), was chosen speaks to the success and impact of Windsor-Smith's story. It remains a core part of the Wolverine canon.

One of the unintended legacies of Windsor-Smith's *Weapon X* may be its influence on the evolution of how Marvel reprints and repackages its archives. *Weapon X* was published before graphic novels became the dominant commercial print format for comics in America. As a result, its perennial reprinting and repackaging over the past three-plus decades has resulted in varying degrees of critical response. After negative feedback on previous editions' coloring, Marvel responded by adjusting the colors of 2021's *Wolverine: Weapon X Gallery Edition* in an effort to present a more attractive collected edition of *Weapon X*. It quickly sold out and was well-received by fans.

This ongoing dialogue about production is vital to the future of Marvel's and many other publishers' archival, art, and reproductive printing.

Other noteworthy details of the *Gallery Edition* include non-glossy paper and a larger-than-standard size designed to show off the details of Windsor-Smith's art. It also collects Windsor-Smith's five pages from *Wolverine* 166, *Uncanny X-Men* 205 (Wounded Wolf), and sixteen pages of reproductions of Windsor-Smith's original art. A standard sized paperback edition of this book followed.

Two European editions have been published in black and white—a Dutch edition (2022) and a French edition (2024).

The edition that comic art fans and I personally long to see is an Artist's Edition. Artist's Editions represent original comic art in fine reproduction at actual size. *Weapon X* marks a highpoint in Windsor-Smith's illustrious career. The best way to appreciate and celebrate this achievement would be to see his original artwork reproduced in high-quality. His color guides should also be included in the Artist's Edition as they are a work of art in themselves and a unique historical artifact of comic book coloring.

While working on this book, I kept thinking of the cyberpunk elements of *Weapon X*. Assuming Windsor-Smith began working on *Weapon X* in 1988 (when it was first mentioned in *Comic Shop News*), the creative period overlaps

Using stat for this page.

Marvel® Comics ILLUSTRATION QUALITY PAPER FOR REGULAR COMIC PAGES

Book Chapt. 13. W-X Issue # 84 pg # 8

Lettering: stat into negative

8

Masamune Shirow's cyberpunk manga masterpiece *Ghost in the Shell* (originally published in serial form 1989–1990). Both books deal with consciousness. Both characters are part of the military/police/intelligence. In Shirow's story, Major is a cyborg. In *Weapon X*, Logan is modified with adamantium added to his bones. He may not be labeled a cyborg, but he looks like one in *Weapon X*. Both characters are violated by people trying to control their minds and bodies. Like *Weapon X*, *Ghost in the Shell* continues to enjoy success from readers and fans as well as through other media adaptations and sequels.

The final part of *Weapon X*'s legacy is its extraordinary quality. Larry Hama recognized this quality in 1993 when he wrote the introduction to the collection. His introduction focuses on this "rare example of real comic book artistry..." Throughout his text, Hama praises what Windsor-Smith does with the comics art form. Hama concludes that "the entire story has a cohesion and structural integrity that is impossible to achieve with the usual collaboration of writer/penciler/inker/colorist/letterer, where every person in the chain is adding a personal interpretation to the pages as they are passed along to him or her along with comments from the editor." This ability to achieve and communicate a singular vision has long been a strength of comics from the early days of Sunday broadsheets to the underground and alternative comics of the 1970s–1990s, and today in original graphic novels and manga that often feature one primary creator.

Windsor-Smith found a way to work at Marvel, outside of their traditional assembly model. His success opened the door for others to try their hand at more personal, non-house style comics. It was a model of how Marvel's characters could be pushed in new directions by trying new approaches to the creative process. Examples of this approach include things like *Omega the Unknown* by novelist Jonathan Lethem and artist Farel Dalrymple; the *Grand Design* series by Ed Piskor, Tom Scioli, and me; and the licensing of characters for projects like Patrick McDonnell's graphic novel the *Super Hero's Journey* or Alex Ross' *Fantastic Four: Full Circle*. Windsor-Smith's success with *Weapon X* is both an inspiration to many creators and a fan favorite for multiple generations.

In revisiting *Weapon X* to write this book, I was surprised by how well it reads. The artwork was never in question. But the story continues to work. It might read better today than when it was originally published. At the time of its publication, I remember feeling like the story was unclear. Part of the reason for that could be due to its serialization. Reading short chapters over the course of six months meant forgetting some details. I also think that my ability to read and comprehend comics has evolved over the last 35 years. Part of this is due to the evolution of the art form. Windsor-Smith's narrative choices were advanced, especially for a Marvel comic in 1991. But the rise of graphic novels, the proliferation of manga, and the growth of the comics form and language has led to more sophisticated storytelling. *Weapon X* was ahead of its time in 1991. I'm reminded of the late, great cartoonist Jack Kirby. He was a visionary, and often his work included radical science fiction and social concepts. He once said that he tried to limit the science fiction in his comics to 30 years in the future. If he went any further, he worried about losing or confusing his audience. As time passed, his work became more readable. His ideas made more sense. Some of the science fiction felt less like science fiction and more like reality. *Weapon X* shares this timeless quality—from Windsor-Smith's auteur creative approach to science fiction and conspiratorial themes that have become mainstream. Of course, the artwork was always and remains breathtaking.

ILLUSTRATIONS

ABOUT THE AUTHOR

Jim Rugg is an Eisner and Ignatz Award-winning cartoonist, designer, zinemaker, and illustrator. His books include *Hulk Grand Design* (2022), the *Street Angel* series, *the PLAIN Janes* (2020), *Octobriana 1976* (2020), *Supermag* (2013), and *Afrodisiac* (2010). He is the co-creator of YouTube's Cartoonist Kayfabe channel. His comics are part of the Smithsonian permanent collection and the National Archives and he taught visual storytelling at the School of Visual Arts and the Animation Workshop in Denmark. Rugg lives and draws in Pittsburgh.

MARVEL AGE OF COMICS

Explore the series!

www.bloomsbury.com/marvel-books

Doctor Strange: A Decade of Dark Magic
by Stuart Moore

The story of one of Marvel's most bizarre, otherworldly heroes, beginning with his creation at the hands of Stan Lee and artist/plotter Steve Ditko, and discussed against the backdrop of one of the most turbulent decades in American history.

Daredevil: Born Again
by Chris Ryall

A smart, meticulous look into the compelling and original storyline of *Daredevil: Born Again*, its gorgeous and unique artwork, and its overall influence in the decades since its release.

The Mighty Avengers vs. the 1970s
by Paul Cornell

The Avengers was **the** comic book of the 1970s. From Civil Rights to Women's Lib, battles for the soul of America became battles between super heroes.

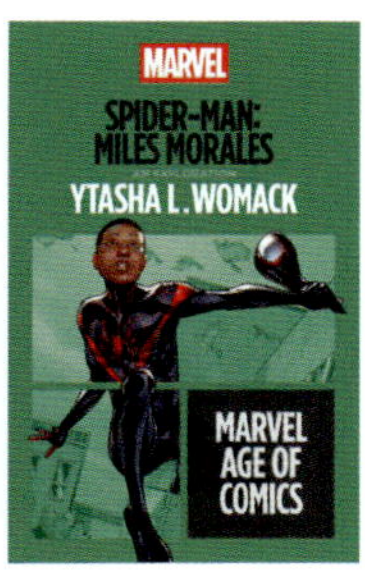

Spider-Man: Miles Morales
by Ytasha L. Womack

A look at the hugely successful reimagining of one of the most popular super hero characters of all time.

The Ultimates
by Ted Adams

The 1990s and early 2000s were a time of intense change and experimentation for Marvel Comics. Out of this emerged *The Ultimates*—a comic which would have an explosive impact on Marvel and the broader pop culture landscape.